53683

S0-BKX-651

The COUNTRYMAN

Through the Seasons

The COUNTRYMAN

Through the Seasons

Johnny Scott

Quiller

We are indebted to *The Field* for its kind permission
to reproduce material originally appearing within its pages.

Copyright © 2019 Johnny Scott

First published in the UK in 2019
by Quiller, an imprint of Quiller Publishing Ltd

British Library Cataloguing-in-Publication Data
A catalogue record for this book is available from the British Library

ISBN 978 1 84689 297 4

The right of Johnny Scott to be identified as the author of this work
has been asserted in accordance with the Copyright, Design and Patent Act 1988.
The information in this book is true and complete to the best of our knowledge. All
recommendations are made without any guarantee on the part of the Publisher, who also
disclaims any liability incurred in connection with the use of this data or specific details.

All rights reserved. No part of this book may be reproduced or transmitted in any form or
by any means, electronic or mechanical including photocopying, recording
or by any information storage and retrieval system, without permission
from the Publisher in writing.

Printed in the Czech Republic

Quiller

An imprint of Quiller Publishing Ltd
Wykey House, Wykey, Shrewsbury, SY4 1JA
Tel: 01939 261616
Email: info@quillerbooks.com
Website: www.quillerpublishing.com

Contents

Introduction

This book consists of a selection of the monthly articles I have written for *The Field* magazine over the years and contains a mixture of topics including sport, natural history, wildlife, customs, traditions, folklore and the heritage of our countryside. It is perhaps more in the nature of a scrap book, in which I have recorded odd episodes and incidents that occur as the wheel of the seasons turns. In one way or another, the subjects I have written about have captured my imagination or been a source of interest to me since early childhood.

The seeds of my fascination with nature were sown on early afternoon walks as a child with my mother, through the ancient coppiced woodland of my father's farm. These walks were not just for the good of my health; post-war rationing was still in place and my mother always carried a wicker basket and, depending on the time of year, filled it with flowers, edible plants, mushrooms, berries or nuts. Trailing along behind her as she foraged, I quickly learnt what was poisonous and what was edible; where to look for it; and why and when it grew there. At the same time, an inquisitive child surrounded by birdsong, darting insects, fluttering butterflies and the furtive rustling of unseen little creatures could scarcely avoid taking an interest in wildlife.

In the 1950s, I think the nation as a whole knew more about the natural history of Britain than at any other time. Rationing, which had started in 1939 and did not end until 1954, meant that for fifteen years the population had to become expert foragers if they wished to supplement their diet. My mother and I often came across others bent on the same mission as ourselves, searching for edible or medicinal plants and collecting firewood. This was particularly the case in the autumn when urban-dwellers poured out of the towns to harvest the hedgerows, searching for vitamin-C-rich blackberries, wild raspberries and rosehips. Traditionally, 14th September was Nutting Day, when coachloads of townspeople would descend on the countryside to strip the hazel trees of nuts – an important extra source of protein through the winter months.

Once I was old enough to roam about unattended, all children of my age had one thing in common, regardless of background: the natural world was our principal source of daily entertainment. After breakfast in virtually every household up and down the country, whether it was urban or rural, the command 'now out you go', would be heard. To be outside, whatever the weather, was considered a healthy, beneficial and profitable way for the young to spend their time. Urban children learnt about natural history in city parks, railway embankments, churchyards and canal banks, whilst rural ones had the freedom of the countryside.

We spent hours being eaten alive by midges, silently watching a badger sett when a sow brought her piglets out at dusk, or a vixen's earth when she played with her cubs on a summer's evening. We kept hedgehogs, grass snakes and talking jackdaws as pets and ferrets for rabbiting. We learnt the breeding seasons of birds, animals, reptiles and insects: we knew the ones that hibernated and those that were nocturnal. We noted the predators and the predated, as well as the corridors of safety, such as hedgerows, which the vulnerable used as habitat or to move between areas of woodland.

In time, we discovered how to read the weather from the behaviour of insects, birds or farm animals and could identify the presence of wildlife. We learnt to interpret clues such as the narrow tracks of rabbits leading from burrow to feeding ground, the broader path of a badger and the slim, four-toed pad mark of a fox. Similarly, we observed the oblong droppings of a rat, the long crinkly ones of a hedgehog, glinting with remnants of undigested beetle carapaces; the twisted dung of a fox, full of bone fragments, fur and seeds, and the acrid urine scent where he marked his territory; the stinking, fishy pile of an otter spraint on a rock beside a river, or the khaki-coloured droppings of a roe deer. Above all, we learnt that wild animals rely on scent and sound to warn them of danger and that silence and a downwind approach were crucial if we hoped to watch them.

My father hunted, fished, stalked, shot and, at least once every season, set off for a week's wildfowling to the Tay, Montrose Bay, the River Kent where it flows into Morecambe Bay, or to Lindisfarne on the Northumberland coast. As I grew older and became more involved in the adult world, I learnt about the different seasons for quarry species, which allow them to breed and rear their young in peace.

My teachers were the wildfowlers, gamekeepers, stalkers, ghillies and Hunt servants I met through my father. From them I discovered the purpose, customs, rules, etiquette, group terms and peculiar language of field sports; the migratory movements of waterfowl; the history, courtesies and consideration of mankind's benign management of wildlife; and, above all, the role of field sports in contributing to the architecture of the landscape by creating, preserving and maintaining habitat for game species, which in turn benefits all biodiversity.

I am very fortunate to have spent my adult life farming hefted hill sheep on the moorlands of the Scottish Borders, an archaic form of farming, which apart from advances in veterinary science, has remained unchanged since the Cistercian monks established great flocks on the uplands of northern England and southern Scotland in the eleventh century. I love the broad perspective, the chuckle of grouse, the seasonal comings and goings of the migratory nesting birds – the snipe, curlew, sky larks, oyster catchers and plovers, who break the long silence of winter with their exuberant birdsong in the spring. Hill sheep are practically wild animals and to farm them at all on the bleak, unfenced uplands a shepherd needs to be a naturalist as much as a stockman.

Dramatic changes have happened to the rest of rural Britain since the arcadia of my childhood, when its largely self-supporting family farms were made up of deciduous woodland shelter belts, orchards, ponds, little fields surrounded by plump hedgerows and old, permanent pastures full of wild flowers.

Characteristically, these were operated as mixed farming systems of sheep, cattle and grain, with chickens, ducks, geese and a fattening pig for bacon. However government policies in the 1960s and 1970s of agricultural intensification led to thousands of miles of hedgerows, small woodland and orchards being bulldozed. Old pastures, heath and downland were ploughed up and marshes drained under Ministry of Agriculture reclamation schemes, which altered much of the rural landscape.

As reclamations destroyed the hedgerows and woodlands, they took with them the tradition of townspeople coming into the countryside to forage and to pick nuts and berries every autumn. Gradually, the urban population began to lose touch with their rural background and as the urban-rural divide widened, so ignorance and prejudice towards country people became part of the political agenda.

Rural Britain will never be quite what it was in my childhood, but then, nothing stands still, however much we may wish it. What is important now, is that the nation is aware of the fragility of what we have left of the beauty and antiquity of our natural heritage and that it must be cherished unaltered.

The countryside should be seen as a force for good: and the communities that live there, their customs and traditions, should be valued and regarded as worth supporting and preserving for future generations.

The wheel of the seasons keeps turning and sometimes, waiting in the dawn on the edge of a saltmarsh for the grey geese to flight inland and looking back across the years, part of a poem written in 1808 by Anna Seward, otherwise known as the Swan of Lichfield, comes to mind:

Nature! dear Parent! Power divine!
Whose Joys and Griefs are truly mine!
To you my sympathy devotes
My cheerful, and my plaintive Notes.

Spring

Toads

There is scarcely a creature in the British Isles, whether it be mammal, reptile, amphibian, insect or bird, which does not change its habits in some noticeable way in March. The winter migrant wildfowl leave for their subarctic homes and little summer visitors such as wheatears, chiffchaffs, willow warblers and yellow wagtails start to arrive. Snipe, curlew, oyster catchers and peewits move from the coast to their upland nesting grounds. Towards the end of the month, early badger cubs may leave their setts; hedgehogs emerge from their hibernation quarters; bumblebees join tortoiseshell, brimstone and peacock butterflies in their search for blossoms, and toads set forth on their laborious annual pilgrimage to their ancestral spawning grounds.

Common toads are our oldest reptile and for a creature so ancient, their reproduction is astonishingly chaotic. Except during the breeding season, both sexes tend to be solitary, living in damp, secluded burrows under logs, rocks or deep in old leaf mould – indeed we have a splendidly warty matriarch who has a lair under a stone water trough by the stables. They usually hibernate in these places alone although occasionally assemble in large groups, sharing a den with snakes and newts, from October to the end of February or whenever the ground temperature reaches a consistent nine degrees centigrade.

In March the toads experience an urge to return to their birth pond to breed, setting off on nocturnal journeys which may take as little as a couple of nights or as long as a month. Ignoring all other ponds and lakes in their path, they tramp steadfastly and with great singleness of purpose towards some pool where their ancestors have bred for centuries, surmounting obstacles such as walls with un-toad-like agility. Unfortunately, many of the hereditary migration routes are now intersected by busy main roads and thousands of toads are squashed by vehicles as they lumber across.

Since the mid-1980s, when the sheer volume of toads killed on the Marlow to Henley-on-Thames road created a serious traffic hazard, several hundred toad tunnels have been built under highways across the country, with flanking walls to guide the convoys of migrants into them. In other areas, volunteers from Wildlife Trusts and the charity, Frogline, monitor likely crossing places, erecting traffic-warning signs and transporting bucketfuls of toads to safety. Despite these efforts, an estimated twenty tons of toads are killed annually. All too often, the survivors' journeys end in disappointment, when they discover that their breeding site has been drained or built over.

When the males finally arrive at the historic breeding area, they wade into the shallows and begin singing their soporific, watery, purring mating call that continues night and day whilst breeding is in progress, unless there is a sharp drop in temperature. Cold makes them torpid and diminishes sex drive, to the extent that the toads all sink to the bottom and bury themselves in the mud until conditions improve. Male toads become sexually active at three years and females, a year later, creating a massive disparity between the males congregating at the breeding sites and available females.

Some of the older male toads cunningly lie in wait and ambush females along the route, arriving at the competitive shambles of the mating areas already clinging to the back of a female with a vice-like embrace – known as amplexus – using the nuptial pads on the inside of their thumbs and fingers. These pads become more pronounced during breeding and provide the grip to enable a male toad to remain in position for hours, and possibly days, whilst his sperm fertilises the female's eggs as they are released. They are also used by competing males to drag each other away from a female or to clamber on to the back of a male already *in situ*. Mating balls or multiple amplexus regularly occur, when several males pile on top of a female, crushing or drowning her. Frustrated, inexperienced young toads frequently mount not only each other but also unsuspecting frogs and even small fish; apart from the mating chorus, the most commonly heard sound throughout the breeding season is the high-pitched, staccato release call of an outraged male.

A female toad will lay as many as two thousand eggs during a successful spawning, which settle in two strings, each about three metres long, round the stems of water plants. Once spawning is over, the adults leave the water and begin the weary, hazardous trudge back to their burrows, no doubt wondering whether it was all really worth it.

The tadpoles hatch after ten days and, although distasteful to most fish, they are prey to water beetles, water boatmen and newts. The tiny golden toadlets metamorphose from tadpoles at between twelve and sixteen weeks, depending on the water temperature. They leave their birth sites in July and August, dispersing into the surrounding countryside to find their own feeding territories.

Toads can live for twenty years in the wild or up to forty in captivity, but the casualty rate is phenomenal. Their only defences against predators are the paratoid glands containing cardiac glycosides – potentially strong enough to stop a heartbeat – that project in the form of lumps at the back of the neck and a disgusting-tasting toxic substance which hyperactivates the salivary glands of anything that tries to bite them, as generations of my terrier pups have discovered. The barely developed paratoid glands of young toadlets offer little protection and thus they are vulnerable to predation from all ground predators, as well as herons, crows and gulls. Sadly, the survival rate is only about one in twenty.

Easter

In AD 595, Pope Gregory sent a mission to England of forty monks, led by a Benedictine called Augustine – Prior of the Abbey of St Anthony in Rome and later the first Archbishop of Canterbury – with instructions to convert the pagan inhabitants to Christianity. Augustine was advised to allow the outward forms of the old heathen festivals and beliefs to remain intact, but wherever possible to superimpose Christian ceremonies and philosophy on them.

The sheer scale of the task confronting the little band of missionaries was so colossal that halfway along the long trudge from Rome they got cold feet and decided to turn back. They were only too aware, leaving seasonal festivals aside, that pagan Britons believed every plant, tree, spring, stream, rock or hill and all animals had souls, and each had its own guardian deity. Before a tree could be cut down, a stream dammed, a mountain crossed, a spring drunk from or an animal disturbed, the individual guardian spirit had first to be placated. Needless to say, every aspect of the wind and the weather had its own gods or goddesses too. Pleas for permission to return were refused and, two years later, the anxious group of monks arrived in Canterbury and began endeavouring to carry out their evangelical papal directives.

Pope Gregory's mandate of conversion through coercion was brilliant in its simplicity; he surmised that the easygoing but deeply superstitious Saxon peasant population would not object if the seasonal festivals of the pagan calendar were Christianised, provided that the ancient celebrations remained basically unchanged. Gradually, the principal heathen feasts became days honouring either Christ himself or one of the Christian martyrs: and the Church had plenty of saints in hand, ready for any eventuality that might arise.

Over several centuries all the pagan days of weather prediction throughout the year – at least forty of them – were given the names of various saints and the principal pagan feast days were converted to Christian religious festivals. Imbolc, held on 2ⁿᵈ February to celebrate the first sign of new growth and the beginnings of lactation in ewes, became Candlemas Day, the Feast of the Purification of the Virgin: Lughnasadh, on 1ˢᵗ August, the celebration of the start of the harvest, became Lammas or St Peter in Fetters Day, when bread baked from the new crop was blessed. The great festival of Samhain, on 31ˢᵗ October, marked the end of the 'light' or growing half of the year and the start of the 'dark' or dead half: pagans believed that the spirits of their ancestors became active with nightfall at Samhain, a superstition substantiated by the ghostly movements of migratory woodcock, or geese flying under the moon. The early Christian Church was quick to designate this All Souls Night and the following day, All Saints Day. The twelve-day festival of Yule at the end of December became the celebration of Christ's birth.

However one festival was so ancient, and so deeply entrenched in the pagan psyche, that although it was to become the most important and defining event of the ecclesiastical calendar, the Church did not attempt to change the name: Easter.

The Holy Scriptures tell us that the crucifixion and resurrection of Jesus occurred around the time of the Jewish Passover festival, which would equate to our spring, with Easter established in western Europe by the First Council of Nicea in AD 325 as being the first Sunday after the full moon following the vernal equinox on 20ᵗʰ March. The spring equinox, when day and night are of the same length and the date from which the hours of sunlight become progressively longer, had been celebrated as a joyous festival of fertility, regrowth and new birth by early civilisations who worshipped their various gods and goddesses in the dawn sunrise for many millennia before the birth of Christ. The Anglo-Saxons worshipped the goddess Eostre, referred to by the

Venerable Bede in chapter fifteen of *De Temporum Ratione* (AD 725), in which he describes the indigenous month names of the English people:

> *Eosturmonth has a name which is now translated to 'Paschal month', and which was once called after a goddess of theirs named Eostre, in whose honour feasts were celebrated in that month. Now they designate that Paschal season by her name, calling the joys of the new rite by the time-honoured name of the old observance.*

There has been a considerable history of suggestion that the goddess Eostre was an invention of Bede's, since very little is known about her other than Bede's attestation. A body of opinion theorising against her existence still has a degree of popular cultural prominence today, although the evidence in his favour is compelling.

Bede was born in AD 672 during the early stages of the Christianisation of these Islands, when the names of the Anglo-Saxon gods and goddesses would have been common knowledge and as the philologist Jacob Grimm (1775-1863), folklorist Charles Billson (1858-1932) and, more recently, Professor Venetia Newall have observed, the highly respected Father of English History would be unlikely to invent a goddess of that name if none had existed. Furthermore, a number of English place names of Saxon origin, such as Eastry in Kent, Eastrea in Cambridgeshire and Eastringham in Yorkshire are assumed to be derived from Eostre. There is also an etymological link to Ostara or Austra, the spring goddess worshipped by the tribes of northern Europe after whom the month of April, Ostermonat, was named and whose existence was verified in 1958, when over 150 Romano-Germanic votive inscriptions to the *matronae Austriahenea* were discovered near Morken-Harff in Germany, datable to around AD 150-250.

The modern imagery of Easter, the eggs and the Easter bunny, pre-date Christianity and have their provenance as pagan fertility symbols, with the bunny originally being a hare. No other animal is surrounded by such a volume of myths, legends, superstitions and omens over so many cultures than is the hare, which is hardly surprising since it is a very unusual animal. Solitary and crepuscular, except in the spring when the bucks and does perform their elaborate mating rituals, hares are capable of speeds up to twenty-five mph, can turn on a sixpence in full flight and jump over twenty feet in the air with ease. This in itself was enough to command the respect of early people, but their behaviour, which sometimes appears almost humanly irrational as they double back and forth in the dusk making sudden leaps and ninety-degree turns, and the hideously childlike screams when caught or injured, convinced our ancestors that hares were more than mere animals.

For many centuries, there was a belief that hares were hermaphrodite and that both sexes bred; that as well as having normal teats on their stomach, they had another set inside their wombs; and that fur grew in their mouths. Although this was eventually disproved in the nineteenth century, hares are almost unique in their extraordinary ability to be pregnant and conceive at the same time, thus carrying two or more foetuses at different stages of growth. This, and their habit of producing four litters in a year, made them worthy of deifying and an obvious symbol of fertility and springtime fecundity.

Some folklorists claim that hares carried the light for Eostre as she lit the spring dawn and although there is not a shred of evidence to support this, it is not unreasonable to agree with the statement written by Charles Billson, the folklorist, in a learned paper on the Easter Hare:

> *... whether there was a goddess named Eostre, or not, and whatever connection the hare may have had with the ritual of Saxon or British worship, there are good grounds for believing that the sacredness of this animal reaches back into an age still more remote, where it is probably a very important part of the great Spring Festival of the prehistoric inhabitants of this island...*

Paradoxically, hares, the wildest and most sensitive of all animals, can be easily tamed if caught young enough, and the Celtic ruling classes liked to keep them in their homes as a sort of living connection to the gods. Boadicea is reputed to have careered into battle on her chariot with the family pet stuffed up her blouse. Caesar remarked that although considered an aphrodisiac by the Romans – Pliny the Elder recommended a diet of hare to increase sexual attractiveness and claimed hare meat had the power to cure sterility – the Celts regarded the flesh of hares as taboo, which gives rise to the perplexing Easter hare-hunting rituals which seem to bear the stamp of immemorial antiquity. Once held in various parts of Leicestershire and Warwickshire, these were believed by the antiquary and politician Charles Elton QC, MP (1839-1900) to be survivals of sacrificial rites connected with the worship of the goddess Eostre.

Perhaps the strangest of all unexplained connections between hares, paganism and Christianity, is the iconography in early medieval churches and cathedrals throughout Britain, depicting three running hares joined by the tips of their ears to form a triangle. This symbolism is found in sacred sites from the Middle and Far East, across Europe and Russia, to places as diverse as St David's Cathedral in Pembrokeshire, Chester Cathedral, a chapel at Cotehele in Cornwall and churches at Widecombe in Devon and Scarborough in Yorkshire.

Eggs have been a symbol of spring rebirth since antiquity. Engraved ostrich eggs have been discovered in Africa dated to sixty thousand years ago; decorated eggs were commonly placed in the graves of ancient Sumerians and Egyptians five thousand years ago, and 'pysanky', the Ukrainian art of elaborately decorating eggs for Easter with beeswax, dates to ancient, pre-Christian times. The custom of colouring Easter eggs was started by the early Christians of Mesopotamia, who dyed their eggs red to represent the blood of Christ, but were only officially adopted by the Church as representing the resurrection in 1610, when Pope Paul proclaimed the following prayer:

Bless, O Lord we beseech thee, this thy creature of eggs, that it may become a wholesome sustenance to thy faithful servants, eating it in thankfulness to thee on account of the resurrection of the Lord.

The two symbols of fertility, the egg and the hare, come together in the ancient German tradition of a mythical hare which laid coloured eggs in its form for good children to find on Easter Day. This was taken to America in the eighteenth century by German immigrants and as Easter gradually became commercialised, the hare became a rabbit and the egg became chocolate.

The Cuckoo

Of all the territorial birdsong heralding the approach of spring in this part of the world – the silly yelping of oyster catchers, the whistling of green plover, the lovely burbling song of curlews and the drumming of snipe – none has greater significance than the call of a cock cuckoo. It is not just that he has customarily always been the harbinger of the season of re-growth and new life: his presence also indicates that insect-eaters such as swallows, house martins and whinchats are not far behind and that means warm weather, desperately needed for grass growth, is bringing them north. There are traditional dates for the arrival of the cuckoo on his journey from Africa: in the South of France, cuckoo watchers expect to hear him on 21st March and his progress is reported across Europe to Norway, where he is due to arrive on 14th April. He should make a landfall in Sussex on the same date, be heard in Cheshire the following day, Worcestershire five days later, Yorkshire on the 21st and is anxiously listened for in the Scottish Borders at the start of the hill lambing on the 24th.

At a time when both the rural economy and people's existence in general were more directly connected to the seasons, the coming of spring and timing of warmer weather was of universal interest. Early people believed cuckoos brought the spring with them and that once the first cock bird's mating call had been heard, everything would spring into life. For many centuries it was the custom in various parts of Britain for farm workers to be given the day off when the first cuckoo of the year was heard. Cuckoo Day was celebrated by drinking new brewed ale known as 'cuckoo ale' and the singing of endless renditions of this little thirteenth century sonnet:

Summer is a-coming in,
Loudly sing, cuckoo!
Grows the seed and blooms the meadow,
And the woods spring new. Sing cuckoo.

Even to-day, the arrival of the cuckoo has lost none of its impact and the date and time the first cock bird's song is heard is still religiously reported in *The Times*. The historical importance of cuckoos is reflected in the sheer quantity of place and plant names, poetry, farming rhymes and folklore. In 1912, the composer Delius was even moved to write a rather lovely lyrical piece about the bird, entitled 'On Hearing the First Cuckoo in Spring'.

It is hardly surprising that cuckoos have attracted so much attention; they are by any standards the most extraordinary birds. The Common Cuckoo, which visits us in the spring, is one of fifty-nine species of *Cuculidae* recognised as being brood parasites and although regarded by us as a national institution, cuckoos are in fact the thoroughly deceitful spongers of the bird world. They not only choose to dump their offspring on little birds because they have a more highly developed mothering instinct than larger ones, they cause their victims' own broods to be destroyed.

Hen cuckoos arrive a week or two after the cocks and whilst he delivers the familiar two-tone territorial call, either from a perch in a tree or on the wing, she hunts the adjacent hedgerows and spinneys for potential host nests, occasionally giving her own, seldom heard, bubbling chuckle in reply. Foster-parents are usually meadow pipits and dunnocks, followed by reed warblers and pied wagtails, but cuckoo eggs have been found in the nests of over fifty different species. Most birds lay in the early morning and the sight of a host bird laying her eggs is sufficient stimulation for a cuckoo to produce one of her own by the afternoon, when the host parents are generally away from the nest. The hen cuckoo lifts an egg from the nest and holds it in her bill whilst she lays her own, which, by some inexplicable process, mimics the colouring and pattern of her victim. The stolen egg is then eaten or destroyed. About forty-eight hours later she identifies another unfortunate target and lays again, repeating the process across her territory until as many as twenty eggs have been deposited in different nests, extending her destructive influence over a large area.

Whatever species the cuckoo chooses to inflict her egg on, it has such a short incubation period – twelve or thirteen days – that it hatches at the same time or before the clutch of the host. The cuckoo nestling is born with a sensitive hollow in its back which it instinctively uses to heave the eggs or nestlings of the host birds out of the nest. Left alone, the nestling grows to such a size that it soon overflows the nest and the tiny, demented foster-parents, struggling to feed the monstrous invader, are often forced to stand on its back. At about three weeks it fledges and then squats on a nearby branch where the hunger cries of a young cuckoo are so incessant that not only will its foster-parents feed it, but also other birds passing by carrying food for their own broods.

By June the cock bird's call changes from a two- to a three-tone song and in July both adults depart, their purpose fulfilled. Their brief visit is reflected in the nursery rhyme:

> *In April come he will,*
> *In May he sings all day,*
> *In June he changes his tune,*
> *And in July he flies away.*

A cuckoo's plumage is blue-grey with barred underparts and their disappearance was once accounted for by the belief that from August until April they turned into the sparrow hawks they closely resemble. Young birds begin the migration journey in August or September, finding their way to their winter quarters in southern Africa unaided, guided by some remarkable inherited directional instinct.

Around twenty thousand pairs breed in Britain every year, but numbers are dropping in tandem with the decline of meadow pipits and dunnocks; a situation to which, bizarrely, they themselves have contributed.

Avian Squatters

Spring in the uplands is a glorious time of year; a warm day or two and suddenly everything comes to life. The long silence of winter is broken by an energising bustle of activity and birdsong, as summer-nesting migrants start arriving from the coast. The wild, ululating territorial call of cock lapwings can be heard as they perform their tumbling, aerobatic display flights. Curlews hang like crescent moons as they circle the breeding areas, their soporific whistling rising to a crescendo that fades away to a strange burbling sound when they dive. Oyster catchers patrol up and down, yapping hysterically. Redshanks yodel; skylarks warble; little stonechats and whinchats hiss and tick. Cock grouse grumble and snipe, plunging through the air with their tail feathers extended, create a weird, mournful, bleating sound.

On a knowe behind our farm buildings is a small wood of old Scotch pines, larches, birch, ash and oak trees. The nesting bird life here is different, but no less frenetic and noisy. Tiny, pugnacious goldcrests, Britain's smallest bird, flicker among the tops of conifers building intricate, expanding nests of spiders' webs, moss and feathers. Tree creepers scuttle up and down like feathered mice, uttering high pitched squeaks. Siskins announce their mating territory with a sweet, fluting twitter. Coal tits trill plaintively. Long-tailed tits splutter shrilly and goldfinches tinkle. Periodically, above this cacophony of exuberant small birdsong, the protracted drumming of our resident greater spotted woodpecker can be heard.

Strangely enough, it is familiar garden birds that have learnt to live in the proximity of humans whose peculiar nesting habits prove the most interesting, particularly to children. The old steading at the back of the house, with its cattle byres, granary and stabling, provides ideal breeding sites for a variety of birds, most of whom gladly utilise manmade objects as part of their home building. Last year, a pair of barn owls made their nest – a disgusting mess of disgorged pellets – on a ledge in the granary, using a section of clay drainage pipe (that must have lain there for decades) as a retaining wall, to stop the owlets falling off. Further along the same ledge, a hen blackbird built a tidy nest of dry grass, leaves and mud in a rusty tin half-filled with nuts and bolts. In the tack room below, where the sheepdogs have their kennels, a pair of dainty pied wagtails reared their brood in a nest of hair and wool in a corner of the wall head.

It would seem that the smaller, more pugnacious and territorial the bird, the more indiscriminate the nest site. Blue tits, the comic little tit mice of poetry, will nest in practically any cavity away from the ground, hissing with fury at any intruders; the only requirement seems to be an unimpeded flight path and enough room to rear their clutch of between seven and twelve eggs.

Holes in a wall or tree are favourite places, but I have known nests in drainpipes, flower pots, a milk bottle stuck in a hedge and even the tool box of a derelict tractor. For several years in succession, a pair nested inside a narrow-necked stoneware jug in a bramble bush that was growing out of an old rubbish dump.

Little skulking wrens with their piercing, rattling song are notorious for choosing strange nesting sites. The cock makes a series of bell-shaped nests for the hen to choose from and will site them in any situation round the house or farmyard where there is any semblance of an entry hole. Proximity to humans doesn't bother them and I have found wrens nesting in a broken carriage lamp among the ivy beside our front door: the coils of a garden hose hanging from a nail: a gym-shoe on a shelf in the summer house: and a crash helmet in the garage. Wrens build their nests with astonishing speed too; years ago, the gardener put his trilby down in the greenhouse when he came to work and found a partially constructed wren's nest in the crown that evening.

Providing nesting sites for little birds can be enormous fun. When my children were small we always had an annual nest-creating day in early March. The children and their little friends scoured the farm for suitable receptacles.

Every farm has a junk heap of considerable antiquity with its ubiquitous elder tree: and the children would return triumphantly with all manner of pots, tins, jars, old kettles, teapots and the occasional hob-nailed boot. With this treasure trove piled into a wheelbarrow, we would set off round the farm pushing his or her find into wall cavities and hedges or fixing them to the branches of trees. How these were positioned was crucial to their eventual occupation, as they had to be rigidly secured, with enough shade, cover and height to give a sense of safety. When checked at the beginning of April, at least half had a blue tit, great tit, wren or robin *in situ*.

Robins claim the most unusual recorded nesting site. The corpses of two highwaymen, executed in 1796 for robbing a mail coach, were hung in gibbets on the green at Mickle Trafford, not far from Chester racecourse. When the remains were finally taken down in 1820, a robin's nest of moss, wool and hair was found in one of the skulls. Our national bird can always be relied upon to provide entertainment in the spring, vociferously establishing mating territories and fighting off all-comers. Hens will cling to a nest under circumstances that would be unthinkable for any other bird.

Over the years, an enormous quantity of lumber accumulated in a loft in one of the old farm buildings, including armchairs with the horsehair stuffing bulging through the material and vast ungainly dressers; rusting iron bedsteads; piles of trunks and suitcases filled with moth-eaten clothes; as well as tea chests full of toys and those treasured infant school projects – drawings and little plaster-of-Paris or papier-mâché figures – that one can't bear to throw away. One whole corner was an enormous heap of plastic bin liners containing decades of annual farm accounts.

Last spring, the floor was considered unstable so the loft had to be emptied and the lumber removed elsewhere, which was a fairly major operation involving several people over a number of days. Much of what had gone up with relative ease was lowered down by rope with considerable difficulty. The exception was the black bin liners – these were hurled off the loft to land in a cloud of dust with a satisfying thud. When the job was finally finished, I went to move a tea chest containing a broken, wicker bottle-basket on top of a pile of toys. The chest had been amongst the first to come down. As I approached, something stirred in one of the bottle compartments. A hen robin, her tail feathers bristling erect, was glaring at me from a newly constructed nest.

Gulls' Eggs

Every year, on or about St George's Day, 23rd April, a small van makes an overnight journey from the West Country, arriving in Billingsgate market at C.J. Newnes & Partners, fish merchants and wholesalers, just as dawn breaks. On board are the first of the eagerly awaited new season's gulls' eggs and, by lunchtime, these highly prized delicacies, with their mottled sea-green shells, will be on display in the food halls of Fortnum & Mason and Harrods. They will also be available from specialist butchers, fishmongers and suppliers and on the menus of fashionable restaurants, the clubs of St James's and the dining rooms of the House of Lords. For a season that lasts no more than four or five weeks, these bantam-sized ovoids, famous for their deep orange yolks and translucent, alabaster whites, are at the top of every gourmand's list.

The eggs of black-headed gulls, *Larus ridibundus*, have been harvested for centuries. These noisy, quarrelsome creatures are the most landlubberly of all gulls, with vast quantities of them living and breeding inland. There are around two hundred thousand mating pairs that nest each year in colonies on coastal sand dunes, salt marshes, moorland bogs, inland lakes and reservoirs.

Some of the colonies are huge, historic places such as the great coastal gulleries of south and eastern England – Grassholme reservoir in Teesdale and Coquet Island off the Northumbrian coast, Thriepmuir reservoir in Midlothian, Loch of Kinnordy in Angus and the Alde and Orde estuaries in East Anglia. Hundreds of other gulleries have as few as fifty nesting pairs, such as the one in a bog out on the heather moorland, which used to provide me with a boiling or two every spring when I farmed in the Lammermuirs.

For hundreds of years, gulls' eggs formed part of the staple diet wherever humans had access to a gullery and were regarded as delicacies by those less fortunate. Their reputation spread with the railways and by the mid-nineteenth century they had become all the rage in fashionable Victorian London. They were a valuable cash crop and landlords with a decent-sized gullery considered themselves to be very fortunate. The one at Scoulton Mere in Norfolk, for example, used to produce an annual harvest of twenty thousand eggs; Bemersyde Moss in Selkirkshire, ten thousand; and Gull Island, in the Beaulieu River estuary, more than both of these put together. However, such numbers represented only a fraction of the total quantity of eggs harvested around the country and sent by train to London.

At one time, outside of the London clubs and a few five star hotels, gulls' eggs were only found in the old-fashioned, traditional restaurants such as Wiltons, Rules, Scott's, Bentley's, Sweetings or Sheekey's and traditionally eaten hard-boiled, with just celery salt. The growth of 'New British Cuisine', has broadened the popularity of gulls' eggs and contemporary chefs now serve them in many different ways: with homemade mayonnaise, asparagus and parmesan, or wood sorrel and new potatoes; soft-boiled with flaked wild salmon belly; or, if you can believe it, slow-cooked with new season morel textures, crushed peas and Jabugo ham.

Even at prices which, in some places, can top a tenner an egg, there is no shortage of demand. Steven Downey, through his company Chef Direct, supplies the restaurant trade with up to twenty thousand per season. David Hammerson, of Everleigh Farm Shop Ltd, provides around five thousand whilst Allen's of Mount Street will sell as many as ten thousand. Perhaps the largest quantity of gulls' eggs assembled for immediate consumption at any one time is for the annual Gulls' Eggs City Luncheon. In its thirtieth year in 2018, some two thousand eggs are eaten by five hundred city professionals at this enormously successful charity event; previously it raised large sums for Macmillan

Cancer Support and is now doing the same for The Cure Parkinson's Trust.

What is there about this delicacy that exerts such a strong hold over its devotees? I have to admit, I asked myself that question when, as a callow youth, my father felt the moment had come to further my education by taking me to lunch at Wiltons and ordering us half-a-dozen each. How, I wondered, as the old boy peeled the first one, could a boiled egg transport a man legendary for his brevity of speech, to heights of poetic rhapsody?

Until one has actually eaten a gull's egg, it is quite difficult to explain the attraction. Chris Gillard, the head chef at Andrew Edmunds in Soho, eulogises about the exquisite richness of the yolk and the extraordinary intensity of its flavour. According to Emmanuel Landres, the restaurant manager at Le Gavroche, gulls' eggs were held in such high esteem by the Roux brothers that they celebrated them by creating *Oeufs Froid à la Czarine* – poached gulls' eggs on artichoke hearts filled with smoked salmon mousse, with a topping of Oscietra caviar and a slice of smoked salmon.

At Wiltons, as one would expect, they have always believed that gulls' eggs should be savoured unadulterated, hard-boiled with just a little celery salt. I asked Jason Phillips, the general manager, what made them so special: A combination of several things. An entirely unique product, truly wild and one of the great traditional foods of old school English cuisine. A landmark in the seasonal calendar which customers always look forward to and of course, they have an inimical, luxurious flavour. From my own experience, the boiling time is crucial: six minutes is plenty to achieve a yolk which should just be damp in the middle. Any longer than this and the delicate texture and creamy richness is destroyed.

Gulls' eggs are a part of our culinary heritage and should be cherished as such, but there is a huge question mark over how much longer anyone will be able to eat them. Since the Wildlife and Countryside Act of 1981, it has been illegal to take the eggs of wild birds.

There are certain exemptions, permitted under the terms of a General Licence, one of which – the collection of black-headed gulls' eggs for human consumption – was reluctantly included because the egg collectors had a strong case of 'tradition by default'.

Both the harvesting and sale of gulls' eggs require separate licences, issued and strictly supervised by the Department for Environment Food and Rural Affairs (which includes Natural England), in conjunction with the RSPB and other local or national wildlife agencies. Considering that the gull population has increased to the extent that they have become a pest species in some urban areas, with local authorities spending fortunes trying to eradicate them on health grounds, a few licences to collect eggs would scarcely seem to pose a problem. Nothing could be further from the truth. The RSPB adopts the view that there can be no justification in taking wild bird eggs for human consumption and it is forbidden to do so on any of their extensive reserves. This attitude is reflected through the other agencies and the handful of people still involved feel that they operate in the face of considerable bureaucratic hostility.

The issue is so sensitive that where the eggs are harvested and who collects them has become shrouded in secrecy. Apart from one or two gulleries over which landlords have historic rights, virtually all gulls' eggs now come from a massive colony in the south-west, where the gulls nest among the spartina grass on the tidal edge of salt marshes. 'Picking' eggs has customarily been carried out by a few of the local inshore fishermen for whom the practice provided a source of income during the slack period for fish.

There are about twenty-five people who have licences through 'tradition by default', and perhaps eight of these, all over retirement age, are still actively involved in collecting eggs. Existing licence-holders have to renew them annually and although anyone can apply for a new licence, my reluctant informant has never heard of an applicant ever being successful. He believes that officialdom, operating loosely under the banner of wildlife conservation, is determined to kill off an ancient tradition.

The season for collecting eggs is restricted by Defra from 15th April to 15th May and permitted only between daybreak and nine a.m. Effectively, by the time they have sailed out to a landing point, collectors have about an hour in which to harvest eggs. They only pick from nests with a single egg in them, partly because this indicates it has been laid recently and is therefore fresh, but mainly because gulls are like chickens and will always lay a replacement. The eggs are then taken home, individually washed and dried – a fiddly business as the shells are notoriously fragile – packed in cardboard egg trays and taken overnight to C.J. Newnes & Partners in Billingsgate.

Once the season is over, the collectors have one week to fill in detailed daily time-sheets marking the different areas from where eggs have been harvested, and return these documents to the relevant office. Those who fail to do so correctly and by the due date have their licences permanently revoked. This may be typical of a statistic-obsessed government department, but officialdom goes out of its way to make life more difficult by never informing collectors whether their licences will be renewed until just before the season starts. It is hardly surprising that with the restrictions, bureaucracy and an uncertain future, there are no young people prepared to keep the custom going.

The real sadness is that the egg collectors know from their lifetimes' experience of the black-headed gull colonies that taking eggs in the spring benefits the species, rather than endangering it as opponents claim. An enormous number of gulls, nesting on the edge of the marshes, will normally have laid a full clutch of eggs by the last week in April. This coincides with the big spring tides which invariably swamp the nests and destroy the eggs. A gull will not nest again after losing a full clutch, but by taking the first egg which the bird will then replace, egg collectors delay the hatching period until the danger from the spring tides has passed. Furthermore, their presence out on the marshes during the nesting season deters predators. Black-headed gulls are strange creatures and it doesn't take much to make them leave a colony. The gulleries at Ravensglass, Bemersyde Moss, Scoulton and Gull Island are among those that have been abandoned. I am told that once the collectors stop harvesting the eggs, the gulls will go. And that would be a tragedy.

Bumblebees

Anno Domini has finally caught up with Tug, my elderly terrier. The dog whose prowess below ground earned him the sobriquet 'Dyno-Rod' is but a shadow of his former self. Shaky of limb, totally deaf and with one eye clouded over, he spends most of his life asleep in a basket filled with old shooting socks, whimpering and twitching as he dreams of past subterranean encounters. On warm days, he becomes slightly more energised and totters off on some mysterious mission of his own, relying entirely on the direction of wind-borne scents to guide him. Recently, he has taken to hunting voles among the tussocks in the hill park behind the steading. It was here I found him one day, barking hoarsely and wrenching mouthfuls of grass and dead plant litter from a clump of densely packed rushes. A vole would be unlikely to cause such extremes of geriatric outrage but the vibration from a bumblebee nest might well do. I hurried over and grabbed him, not because I was afraid he would be stung but because, like most people, I adore bumblebees.

With the first spring sunshine, young queen bumblebees, fertilised the previous summer, emerge from winter hibernation and drowsily forage for plant nectar. After a couple of weeks, they start actively searching for a nest site – depending on species, the abandoned nests of mice or voles, tussocks or dense leaf litter at the base of hedges. Once a suitable place has been found, the bee makes a circular chamber of fine grass and plant debris. Inside, she constructs a cup with wax secreted from her abdomen, partially filled with pollen, on which to lay her eggs. At the same time another wax vessel is made to store a reserve of honey in case the weather turns cold and she is unable to forage.

Once the eggs are laid, the bee closes the cup with wax, incubates them like a broody hen and nourishes the grubs with honey and pollen once they hatch. Within a month, these emerge as fully-fledged, sterile female worker bees, who feed the queen and the new broods of grubs as she produces them. As summer wears on, the queen lays fewer eggs and with the increase in food provided by the workers, some of the larvae develop into queens themselves, whilst others become drones (male bumblebees). These mate; the little colony disintegrates and all except new queens die as autumn approaches.

There are about two hundred species of bumblebee worldwide and around nineteen in Britain. Six are familiar to most of us: buff-tailed, carder, white-tailed, red-tailed, the early-nesting bee with orange tail, and the yellow-banded garden bee. Some, like the red-shanked, great yellow, shrill carder and blaeberry bumblebees are increasingly rare.

There are also six species of cuckoo bumblebee which, like their avian namesake, are parasites. Emerging from hibernation later than normal bumblebees and invading an established nest to lay their eggs, cuckoo bees resemble the species they intend to use as a host; they enter the nest, stinging the sitting queen to death, and then rely on the existing worker bees to bring up their brood. The progeny are either all fertile females or drones – there are no workers – and their presence defeats the purpose of the original colony as cuckoo grubs use up resources whilst contributing nothing to the nest.

The other major parasite affecting the success of a nest is canopid flies. These lurk in the vicinity of flowers that attract bumblebees and, when a bee is busy and occupied feeding, it leaps out of hiding, and thrusts an egg into the bee's body. The egg feeds inside the bee and kills it within a fortnight.

So essential are bees – and bumblebees in particular – as pollinators of crops, flowers and trees, that according to Einstein if they ceased to exist, mankind could not survive for more than four years. Unlike honey bees, the humble bumble is a hardy beast: the thick hair-covering and ability to dislocate and vibrate their wing muscles to generate body heat enables them to be active earlier in the growing season, when temperatures are below ten degrees centigrade, in wind or when there is cloud cover. Bumblebees are the chief pollinators of the orchards and soft fruit market gardens of northern Europe and Scandinavia. They are much stronger, more aggressive foragers than honey bees, forcing open flowers such as antirrhinum to get at nectar and pollen, which is transferred from plant to plant on their body hairs.

Agriculturalists have been aware of the bumblebee's essential role in pollination since the eighteenth century. Long-tongued species, such as carder, white-tailed, garden and ruderal bumblebees, that can reach into the long, narrow corollas of certain plants, were all imported to New Zealand in 1885 to pollinate red clover and alfalfa forage crops. Bumblebees are now bred commercially for pollinating a whole range of fruit and vegetables cultivated in large-scale greenhouses. Around half a million colonies are reared annually and used in over thirty countries to cultivate everything from strawberries and kiwi fruit, to cranberries, blueberries, aubergines, sweet peppers and cabbages. They are especially important in pollinating tomato plants: tomato flowers are among flora that release pollen through vibration and bumblebees are one of the few species to 'buzz pollinate'. They seize hold of pollen-bearing anthers in the flower's centre and release pollen by vibrating their flight muscles without moving their wings. Bumblebees have now almost entirely replaced the labour-intensive artificial pollination previously used by commercial tomato growers.

Part of the fascination of bumblebees is how, with fat, hairy bodies completely out of proportion to their wings, they defy accepted theories of aerodynamics to become airborne. Bumblebee aeronautics studied at Göttingen University in the 1930s proved that, theoretically, they could not generate enough power for lift-off. The Bumblebee Paradox puzzled and infuriated the world of science until 1996, when the Zoology Department at Cambridge University built robotic models to monitor airflow round moving wing-tips. Over the following decade, researchers discovered that the flexible wings of a bumblebee, when forced through air at an acute angle, create a powerful vortex. Vortices – swirling masses of air – caused by rapid wing-beats produce sufficient up-draught for take-off and keep the bee flying with surprising agility.

Large tracts of the British countryside have altered dramatically since the 1950s and bumblebees have suffered more from habitat destruction than almost any other wildlife. Three species are already extinct – the apple, cullems and short-haired bumblebee – whilst many others have become scarce or localised. Bumblebees are active from spring until late summer and require a variety of different nectar and pollen sources during this period to keep the nest provisioned. Worker bees have a foraging range of under a mile and the loss of a particular flower species within their radius at a crucial time, through pesticides, forestry planting, urban development or changes in farming practice, can spell doom for the colony. What with one thing and another, life for the poor old bumblebee is quite difficult enough without a visit from Tug.

Bugs in May

May is the poet's month; wild flower growth is quite breathtaking, with verges on country lanes gleaming white as wild parsley, stitchwort, white dead nettle and hawthorn come into blossom. Gorse, buttercups, meadow vetchling, cowslips, celandine, dandelions, yellow rattle and bird's-foot trefoil throw a golden sheen across heaths, wood margins and meadows. Woodlands are carpeted in bluebells, clusters of purple-flowered bittersweet, pink purslane, red campion, wood sorrel, blue speedwell, ransoms and sweet woodruff, in their last flush of growth before the leaf canopy closes over them. A haze of yellow, pink or white blossom surrounds laburnum, ash, horse chestnut, crab apple, rowan, sycamore or whitebeam, while in old permanent pasture and damp hollows, ragged robin, poppy, sundew, horsetail and pennywort add a splash of purple, scarlet and brilliant green.

Sometimes, when the temperature drops on a May evening, a warm gust of air passes by, filled with an exquisite scent. A combination of all the day's blossom fragrances, it lasts for a second or two, then the evening chill closes in and a wonder of nature is completely gone. Except in the north, where caution is recommended – 'cast not a clout 'til May is out'– weather lore now becomes generally positive. Some light rain is desired for future fecundity, as in 'rain in May makes bread for the whole year', or 'May showers bring milk and meal'. The Saxon name for May was *Tri-Milchi*, named for the abundance of grass growth which enabled cows to be milked three times a day.

Warmth is the key factor and 'a swarm of bees in May makes a load of hay', is indicative of how important heat in early May was to rural communities. Until the eighteenth century, honey was largely the universal sweetener or preservative and considered as valuable as a good hay crop. Bees swarm to create new colonies and if the weather were warm enough for this to happen, a plentiful supply of honey would be guaranteed for the coming year. Insect life explodes when the temperature rises in May: millions of every conceivable type of bug, beetle, ant, spider, earwig, bee, midge, wasp, woodlouse, slug and snail, crawl, squirm, hop or fly, in a frenzy of activity.

May bugs thump against windows on warm evenings or blunder into the room, drawn to the light in the search for a mate; yellow Brimstone, Peacock, Orange-tip and Speckled Wood butterflies are joined by Adonis, Chalk Hills and Common Blues; brightly coloured dragonflies defend territories on the edges of ponds and lakes; damselflies bind together as they mate, and in clean, fast-flowing streams, where white-flowered, water-crowfoot grows, brown trout rise to the mayfly hatch.

Watching insects can be a fascinating method of forecasting weather. Bees, ants and spiders are our most intelligent insects and their behaviour is absolutely infallible; when ants bustle about in a state of agitation, rain is on the way. Introducing moisture or humidity into a colony would be catastrophic and you will never see an ant out of its nest during rain. If the entrance to an anthill is open, the weather will be fine; if closed, expect wet weather. Watch out if you see ants on the move, lugging eggs with them; they will be abandoning their nest ahead of a flood.

Bees never fly far from the hive if rain is imminent and will swarm only if they are entirely confident the weather is going to remain settled and dry. Observing how and when spiders such as garden, veil-web, comb-footed or four-spotted weave their webs can be a useful weather barometer: 'When spiders weave their webs by noon, Fine weather is coming soon.' High winds can destroy a web and, before a gale, spiders can be seen shortening and strengthening their webs. When frame lines are short and stout, blustery weather is approaching, while long, slender frames are a reliable sign of a calm, clear day. A web needs constant attention and can be replaced every twenty-four hours; if a spider is working on its web on a summer's evening, there will be no rain that night. One seen at work in the morning guarantees the day will be fine.

Insects are a food source to many birds and the height they fly at is indicative of good or bad weather. Swifts, swallows and house martins, swooping round treetops or roofs on a summer's evening, are feeding on insects carried there by thermals created by high pressure, indicating fair weather the next day. If they fly low, it is almost certain to be wet. The same is true of bats hunting in the gloaming or at daybreak. Flying insects, particularly biting ones such as gnats, midges, mosquitoes and horseflies, become more of an irritation before rain. As low pressure approaches, humidity builds up and, with the added weight of moisture on their wings, insects fly lower.

Heat makes people perspire and odours are released when atmospheric pressure on the body lowers, making some humans more than others an obvious target. If the dreaded midge is to be seen dancing up and down vortices in the beams of the setting sun, it will be clear and dry the following day. If they gather sluggishly under trees and bite more than usual, there will inevitably be rain: 'When eager bites the thirsty flea, Clouds and rain you will surely see.'

The Golden Hoof

I once overheard our MFH say to a keen young member of the field, famous for her long legs, blue eyes and innocent smile: 'Now, my dear, you cut along to the far end of this lane and go on point for me at the corner of the wood opposite a field of peculiar looking black sheep.' These I later identified as dark-skinned Zwartbles, big sheep from the cold, wet marshes of northern Holland and yet another Continental breed gaining popularity for hardiness, mothering instinct, tight fleece and resistance to foot-rot. I sympathised with our MFH in not knowing what they were, as there are currently around thirty-five million sheep of various ages in Britain, including sixteen million ewes, made up from more than sixty different breeds and every conceivable permutation of crossbred or mule, which now make up the basis of all commercial lowland sheep systems.

Despite the enormous diversity of landscape, climate, soil and herbage, the British Isles have always been ideally suited to sheep farming. The Celts were exporting raw wool and cloth to Rome, 'so fine it was comparable with a spider's web' before the Roman invasion of 55 BC.

The Romans introduced long-wool breeds from Spain to improve the small, horned, native sheep, establishing a large wool-processing factory at Winchester early in the Occupation and, by AD 100, England and Spain were recognised as the twin centres of wool production in the Western world. The sheep industry collapsed in the chaos following the fall of Rome but, by the eighth century, the Saxons were again exporting wool and the importance of sheep is reflected in place names such as Shepley, Shipley, Sheppey, Shipton, Shipbrook, Ramsdean and Ewesleys. In Saxon Britain, milk for cheese, an important source of winter protein, was the main product of sheep, with wool and manure being valuable by-products. Sheep were the most numerous breed of livestock listed in the Domesday Book.

The Normans, and Cistercian monks in particular, created a sheep industry that became the backbone of the nation's might and prosperity, symbolised by the Woolsack in the House of Lords. The object of the Cistercian Order was simplicity and self-sufficiency, but a surplus of wool from its farming operations, coupled with a huge demand from Continental wool merchants and a desire to build beautiful religious houses, soon led to commercial sheep farming on a massive scale. Vast flocks were established across the uplands of Britain. In Yorkshire alone, sheep belonging to abbeys such as Fountains, Kirkstall, Roche, Byland and Rievaulx are thought to have numbered some quarter of a million, with probably as many again at Cistercian abbeys in the Scottish Borders. Other monastic establishments and many landowners were quick to follow, as Britain gained a reputation among Flemish and Italian merchants for growing the finest wool. By the early fourteenth century, sheep numbers had reached upwards of twenty million. Raw wool was exported to Bruges, the centre of the weaving industry, and re-imported as cloth. However, in 1370, Edward III doubled the value of wool by encouraging Flemish weavers to settle in England, transforming the nascent domestic cloth industry and creating a lucrative export market in woven goods. Many weavers settled in Norfolk and Suffolk, with others moving to the West Country, the Cotswolds, the Yorkshire Dales and Cumberland.

The Church, the land-owning elite and merchants made immense fortunes from wool and bequeathed us magnificent and architecturally stunning 'wool' churches such as St Peter and St Paul's in Lavenham, St Mary's in Bury St Edmunds, St Agnes's in Cawston, All Saints' in Stamford and St John the Baptist's in Burford and Cirencester. From the twelfth to the eighteenth centuries, the prime object of sheep farming was wool production. Milk for cheese and manure for maintaining soil fertility were subsidiary, meat or carcass conformation being almost ignored. When a sheep was too old to produce wool, it was merely fattened for slaughter. Breeds, in the modern sense, did not exist, with sheep classified by the type of wool produced in different parts of the country, which in turn was dictated by regional and nutritional variations in grazing.

Broadly speaking, there were small, horned, white, tan or blackfaced coarse-wool sheep on poor ground throughout the West Country, Wales, the northwest, coastal East Anglia, the Borders and parts of Scotland. A larger, polled, long-wool type was found across the better land in Kent, the Midlands, the Cotswolds, Lincolnshire and into Yorkshire, whilst a dense-fleeced, short wool type was to be found on the downland pastures of the south coast and along the Welsh border counties. This was the most sought-after wool and the best came from the Benedictine monastery at Leominster, the famous Lemster Ore, the golden fleece of England, 'that with the silkworm's thread, the finest doth compare'. Although medieval sheep farmers relied on agricultural improvements and superior grazing to enhance wool quality, both long and dense-wool breeds had their origins in the Roman sheep that survived on the Kent marshes. These animals became the property of the Benedictine Order after it was established at Canterbury in AD 597 and 'Canterbury' sheep would have been taken to newer Benedictine houses as they were founded.

The eighteenth century was a period of rapid change for every section of society but none more so than farmers, facing the challenges of demand created by a rising population, increasing colonisation, a large standing army and a burgeoning distilling industry. Virtually every farmer was caught up in the fever for improvement in crops and livestock, fuelled by escalating food prices. Landlords led the way, with nobles such as Townshend, Egremont, Leicester and Bedford in England, and Graham, Grant, Hamilton and Tweedsmuir in Scotland transforming their estates through drainage and fertilisation. Robert Bakewell of Dishley in Leicestershire and John Ellman of Glynde in Sussex were two of the agriculturalists from that period to have the greatest influence on British sheep breeds.

Carcass conformation was now as important as wool and Bakewell, the foremost exponent of selective breeding, developed the Leicester, a large, long-wooled, fast-maturing sheep. At the same time, John Ellman was transforming the lean, leggy sheep of the South Downs into a squat, compact type that gave excellent mutton yield – mutton being meat from sheep more than than two years of age and preferably older – while retaining a good, dense fleece. The new communication system of roads and canals made quality livestock available to farmers across the country and Bakewell's Leicester improved the old Cotswold and became the progenitor of longwools such as the Devon and Cornwall, Teeswater, Wensleydale, Border Leicester, Lincoln and Whitefaced Dartmoor, while Southdown rams were used on downland breeds to create the Dorset and Dorset Horn, Hampshire, Wiltshire Horn, Oxford Down, Ryeland, Shropshire and the Suffolk. The latter would become the most famous fat-lamb-producing sire in the world.

To accommodate agricultural expansion, Enclosure Acts had been passed in 1760 and continued almost annually for the following century, as more and more common land was enclosed, amounting to at least three million hectares. For the first time since the dissolution of the monasteries, sheep in large numbers were established on the hills of northern Britain, with graziers burning old heather to create palatable regrowth, which ultimately led to the development of grouse moors. It would not have been possible to fence the hills, so early graziers, appreciating the delicate nature of the herbage and its susceptibility to overgrazing, devised a method of 'hefting' the sheep. Each area of hill was assessed for its potential stocking rate and a sustainable number of ewes was established on individual areas of land known as hefts. It was labour-intensive but, by utilising the territorial nature of hill sheep and replacing old ewes with ewe lambs from the same heft each year, knowledge of grazing territories passed from mother to daughter. The sheep of hefted hill flocks today are the lineal descendants of those established three hundred years ago and graze exactly the same ground.

By the 1840s, and for the following hundred years, it was possible to travel the length of Britain and recognise each county by the breed characteristics of its sheep. For example, the big Romneys of Kent; the close-wools of the Home Counties and Welsh borders; the long-wools of the Midlands and the north; and the horned, coarse-wool hill sheep of Exmoor, Lancashire, Yorkshire and Cumberland – Lonk, Dalesbred, Rough Fell and Swaledale. The grey Herdwick thrived in the Lake District and hardy Blackface sheep throughout the heather uplands and Highlands of Scotland. Wales and the Scottish Borders had polled hill sheep – Hill Radnor, White, Black and Balwen Welsh Mountain, Clun Forest, Beulah, Badger Face and Cheviot. Farther north could be found the North Country Cheviot of Sutherland and Caithness. Wool was still a major part of farm income and even on poor hill farms the wool clip was said to pay the rent of a farm or a shepherd's wage; but mutton was of equal importance.

The sheep industry altered dramatically after the Second World War, as man-made fibres replaced wool and eating habits changed. Smaller cuts of lamb became the housewife's choice. The emphasis now was on lamb production, with standardisation dictated by supermarkets requiring a lean lamb ready for slaughter at sixteen weeks.

The perfect ewe to meet these requirements was a crossbred. Ewes drafted from hill flocks as part of the hefting practice – Swaledale, Welsh Mountain or Scotch Blackface, for example – are crossed with a Bluefaced Leicester ram, combining the hardiness and mothering instinct of a hill ewe with the size, prolificacy and milkiness of the long-wool. Their progeny, known as North Country, Welsh or Scottish mules, are put to an outstanding carcass-quality terminal sire such as a Suffolk or Texel, to produce the perfect lamb for today's market.

Our hill sheep are the same as they were two hundred and fifty years ago, and many small flocks of regional breeds still exist, but the half-bred predominates and farmers endlessly experiment to find a ewe that suits their farming system. Thus we also have Romney, Cheviot, Dorset, Clun and Beulah mules, to name but a few. There is even a Zwartbles mule: now that is a peculiar-looking sheep.

Are Sportsmen Getting Soft?

Poking about in the attics recently, I came across a collection of fishing albums containing faded black and white photographs from the 1950s and 1960s, when my parents and grandparents fished at Endsleigh on the Tamar and the Delfur beat on the Spey. Many of them are posed family groups taken outside various fishing huts with rods, gaffs, thumb-sticks and landing-nets in the background, or of individuals in canvas waders and leather hobnailed wading boots proudly holding a fish aloft. One photograph in particular caught my eye: it is of my grandmother, waist-deep in the Spey, casting with her favourite rod, a sixteen-foot Grant's Vibration. This beautiful greenheart rod, made by Playfair, with 'drop-down' rod rings and overlapping joins secured by oiled deerskin straps, weighed more than nine pounds complete with brass reel. Considered a light rod compared with some in use at the time, it is hard to believe that, fifty or more years later, the modern equivalent in high modulus graphite – an Orvis Shooting Star, for example, plus a Battenkill Large Arbor reel – now weighs just under a pound and a half.

Advances in fibre composite technology have made a huge difference right across the spectrum of fieldsports. I remember as a small boy watching in awe as my father assembled the wildfowling kit for his January forays to shoot geese on the Tay estuary. 'You need layers for 'fowling', he told me, as he packed vests made of real string and woollen long-john combinations with buttons at the wrist and ankle, thick flannel shirts, seaman's jerseys, oiled wool socks and corduroy breeches. He also had a sheepskin jerkin known as a 'fear nought' and a hooded canvas smock lined in mungo with a strap that buckled between the legs. Added to these were a balaclava, mittens, rubber thigh-waders with nailed leather soles, a gamebag, thumb-stick and a double 8-bore that weighed twelve pounds and seven ounces. I know, since I still wear much of this gear, that none of it, bar the waders, is waterproof. Not that it matters; the layering is so effective that, regardless of the temperature, I am drenched with sweat in the first fifty yards.

Nowadays, my 'fowling companions claim to be warm and completely dry, inside and out, in their ultra-lightweight polypropylene and cotton undergarments, three-ply nylon and rubber chest-waders and Realtree camouflage jackets made with high-strength, water-resistant DuraSupple lined with an Airmax Thermo fleece bonded to a waterproof membrane. Most of the 'you-can't-see-me' brigade favour three-and-a-half-inch chambered 12-bore semi-automatics weighing about seven-and-a-half pounds and only a handful of big gun romanticists like myself still use the heavy old 8- or 4-bore goose-guns.

The weaving industry has also been revolutionised in the past few decades. My father's generation and its predecessors would never have considered having shooting clothes made in tweed lighter than thirty ounces.

Traditionally, weight meant warmth, weatherproofing and durability, and tweeds were woven accordingly. The cloth was as stiff as a board when new, took ages to 'wear in' and was, in most cases, incredibly uncomfortable, rubbing the inside of legs raw. Its great redeeming feature was that if you were caught on the hill in really foul weather miles from home, you might get soaked and utterly miserable but as long as you kept going, the wool fibres retained body heat and kept out the cold.

The growth of corporate shooting since the 1980s has created a demand for lighter, finer, more supple tweed, though retaining the properties and appearance of heavier, traditional cloth. Specialist weavers such as Lovat Mills in Hawick, the foremost manufacturer of estate tweeds, have combined ancient skills with modern technology to create hard-wearing, lightweight performance tweeds: innovative, contemporary fabrics in high-twist yarn containing lycra or nylon filaments for strength, coated in Teflon for water resistance and made up with Gore-Tex drop liners which allow condensation to travel one way but not the other.

Someone new to fieldsports can even buy cloth that has been decatised to create an antique finish, giving the impression that he or she has had their shooting clothes for years. To a lesser degree, the same is true of hunting clothes. The old Bedford cord breeches, which have to be washed and stretched on a wooden frame to stop them shrinking, and heavy Melton cloth coats that are wonderfully weatherproof but take such a lot of valeting, are being replaced with materials made with nylon for stretch and flexibility and coated with silicone for waterproofing. Wax calf boots (which I actually enjoy cleaning and boning) are being made redundant by high-quality look-alikes in rubber-coated leather at a fraction of the price, and they only require washing off.

Undoubtedly, the greatest change of the past fifty years has been in vehicles and access. As a child, I hacked miles to a meet, hunted all day and hound-jogged home again. The horsebox was used only to get to meets on the far side of the country or if we were hunting with a neighbouring pack.

Every autumn, we went down to Exmoor to hunt with the Devon & Somerset Staghounds and I do not remember ever boxing to a meet. Since the mid-seventies, the increasing volume of traffic on even minor roads has made hacking to meets so unpleasant and potentially dangerous – particularly when coming home – that unless hounds are meeting on the doorstep, we box everywhere. In fact, the only time I have ridden home in recent years – all eight miles of the journey – was when a Fell pony that had boxed with alacrity in the morning for a day in the hills, flatly refused to get back in in the afternoon.

Not that long ago, a stalking party walked to the hill and the respective beats' distance from the lodge dictated the time of departure in the morning. True, there were occasions when a track might be accessible from a public road or by boat, but that was the exception rather than the rule. Now a combination of four-wheel drive and tracked vehicles can take parties at least to the edge of the tree line. On smart driven pheasant and partridge days, fleets of SUVs ferry guns from stand to stand and I doubt that anyone walks more than a hundred yards between drives. There is a well-known grouse moor near here with a line of butts up the side of a steep cleugh known as Cardiac Climb. Once upon a time, there was brisk betting among the loaders, flankers and pickers-up on the length of time it would take a gun to reach the top butt and the number of times he would stop on the way up! It was also not unheard of for money to be exchanged between guns to avoid this lofty position, which could lead to a dramatic shortening of the odds. Now, as on many other moors, guns are delivered to and collected from their butt by Argocat.

So, are modern sportsmen getting soft? Compared with previous generations, I suppose so. As a nation we all take less 'natural' exercise than our predecessors and none of us walks or rides as far as we did because progress has provided alternatives. When I started farming, hill farmers and shepherds 'looked' their sheep by walking the high ground every morning and the low ground every afternoon, wearing 'heather loupers', heavy hobnailed hill boots with turned-up toes. Now, we look our sheep on the quad bikes with which progress has provided us. It is more labour effective, if less pleasant, and we are comparatively softer as a result.

One pertinent observation in favour of progress was put to me by a stalker the other day: 'My laird is getting on and without quads or four-wheel drives, he and our older guests wouldn't be able to enjoy what the estate has to offer.' This point of view was brought home to me when I stopped for fuel at the Tebay service station on the M6 in

Cumbria. A stout, elderly party sporting a very expensive nose was filling a Range Rover which had an Eco Rider (a two-wheeled bike with big, low ground-pressure tyres) attached to the back. 'Got a dicky ticker and me knees have pretty well had it,' he told me. 'Thought I was going to have to give up all the things I love. Bought this bike and now I can get anywhere – right out to the hill, along a bank, to a butt or a peg, follow hounds. Given me a new lease of life.'

Despite political antipathy, fieldsports have become increasingly popular over the past couple of decades. A recent survey shows that shooting supports the equivalent of seventy thousand full-time jobs and that guns spend £2 billion per annum on goods and services, generating £1.6 billion to the economy. Shoots spend an estimated £250 million every year on conservation and are the driving force behind the habitat preservation and management of two million hectares of landscape. Much of this has been possible only through advances in modern technology across a wide range of products. Sportsmen may have become softer but there are now more of them and they are, as a body, much stronger.

May Day

With hill lambing lasting from the middle of April until well into the following month, May Day and the attendant Bank Holiday have played no part in my life for virtually my entire farming career. By and large, I remain unmoved by reports dominating the news of the exodus from towns, chaos on the motorways and speculation about the weather. The exception is the rare occasion when a warm current of air carries the exquisite scent of hawthorn blossom up into the hills. This happens only once every few years but when it does, I have a vivid mental flashback to my childhood home and children dancing round the maypole.

On May Day, my mother always opened the gardens to the public and, as an added attraction, little girls from the village school, wearing long white dresses, were dragooned into performing ribbon dances round a flower-decked pole erected on one of the lawns. They were required to execute increasingly complicated steps whilst the red, white and blue ribbons formed patterns up and down the pole. Beginning with the Single Plait, they then moved through the intricacies of Double Plait, Barber's Pole, Jacob's Ladder and Spider's Web, to finish – their faces creased with concentration – with Gypsy's Tent, the most difficult manouvre of them all.

This enchanting rural scene, repeated in towns and villages all over Britain at the beginning of May, is a relatively modern interpretation of a much more ancient festival. Ribbon dancing became a popular stage act during the eighteenth century, particularly in London's famous pleasure gardens, the Cremorne and Ranelagh. In 1881, it was introduced to Whitelands College, the teacher training college for women, as part of their May Day celebrations, by the Victorian philanthropist and art critic, John Ruskin. The enthusiasm of Whiteland graduates spread the idea to schools throughout Britain, and indeed to much of the English-speaking world, with such success that ribbon dancing round the maypole has become accepted as a May Day tradition.

Celebrating the start of real summer growth is as old as antiquity. On a summit not far from here is a megalithic standing stone, one of many thousands erected across Europe. At this time of year, I like to think of dreamy Bronze Age herdsmen capering round it as dawn broke and the sun came up. Later, Beltane became the most significant festival in the Celtic calendar with Druids lighting great ritual bonfires on hilltops at sundown the previous day.

The Romans marked the start of the new life cycle with a six-day orgy dedicated to Flora, the goddess of flowers and re-growth (as well as the patroness of prostitutes). It was a time of great rejoicing, dancing and merriment. Houses, public buildings and temples were decked with flowers and greenery, collected the previous day, whilst hares, a symbol of fertility, were released into the streets. Enthusiasm for this festival spread across Europe to Britain as the Roman Empire expanded, its customs becoming entwined with those of Beltane and eventually, Walpurgis Night, the fertility celebration of subsequent Norse invaders.

May Day revelries in Britain reached their height during the Middle Ages and were to last for several centuries. The custom of going into the woods and countryside 'a-maying', i.e. gathering flowers, greenery and branches of hawthorn blossom the night before, became synonymous with licentious behaviour, which was enjoyed by all levels of society including the clergy. A 'green wood marriage' or 'to wear a green gown' were well-known euphemisms for what went on under the cover of darkness. Having washed their faces in the morning dew, the returning foragers carried tall saplings back with them and erected these on village greens as the focal points for dancing, games, ceremonies and the selection of May Queens.

Maypoles became a symbol of May Day and were equally as popular in urban communities as in rural ones, with some choosing to erect permanent poles.

Two of the most famous were in London, at Cornhill and the Strand. The Cornhill maypole was so tall that the adjacent church became known as St Andrew Undershaft. However, the pole was cut down in 1517 after the riots of 'Evil May Day', when the London apprentices used it as a rallying point for their attacks on the homes of immigrant workers in the East End. The one in the Strand, erected during the reign of Elizabeth I, came down in 1644. It was a victim of a Parliamentary Ordnance instructing the constables of parishes that 'all and singular maypoles that are or shall be erected to be taken down and removed'.

May Day had long been a target for the zealous reformers of the Protestant Church, with the voices of opposition becoming more strident year by year. To them, May Day was no harmless folk festival; everything about it was pagan and ungodly. It had its origin in ancient fertility rites. Maypoles smacked of tree worship, were possibly phallic in connotation and were certainly idolatrous. The abandoned dancing and raucous merrymaking were a threat to public order. The custom of going a-maying and the associated promiscuity was a revolting moral disgrace. Worse than all of these strictures, May Day personified the evils of social liberalism encouraged by a Roman Catholic monarchy. Thus May Day and many other traditional customs – including Christmas – were outlawed during Cromwell's Commonwealth.

On 1st May 1660, Parliament invited Charles II to return as King and, as a sign of the good times to come, maypoles were re-erected all over the country. To replace the maypole in the Strand, a massive limb forty metres long was floated up the Thames and hauled upright by a team of sailors under the direction of the Duke of York. Painted with gilt and covered with coloured balls and flags, this symbol of rejoicing remained in place for over fifty years before being removed to provide a site for the church of St Mary le Strand. The redundant pole was subsequently bought by Isaac Newton and taken to Wanstead in east London, where the base was used to support Huygens' enormous telescope.

The Restoration saw a return of the old, uninhibited May Day behaviour. London's fifteen-day May fair, held on the site of what is now Curzon Street and Shepherd Market, became so notorious for drunkenness and bad behaviour that it was suppressed in 1708. Revived by popular demand a few years later, the fair was finally banned altogether in the 1770s. May Day celebrations lost their impetus during the Industrial Revolution but were revived by the Victorians – with their passion for 'Merrie England' – in a more genteel and romanticised form.

Nowadays, May Day is all things to all men: it is a public holiday commemorating the international workers' struggle to achieve an eight-hour working day; it is a neopagan festival; it is a commercialised celebration of spring and an excuse for demonstration and political protest. The only thing that concerns hill lambers is the prospect of some warm weather.

Cleanliness of Animals

If you happen to be in the Borders and notice a small, white dog with heavily muscled hindquarters wearing a dirty, once-white lampshade, the chances are that it will be Tug, my elderly terrier. Recently he returned from one of his little excursions covered in earth and smelling of you-know-what, with one eye half closed. The vet diagnosed a scratched eyeball, requiring the inner eyelids to be stitched together and a plastic funnel to encase his head, preventing him from rubbing the stitches loose. Needless to say, this is not the first time such a precaution has been necessary and I know from experience that wearing the funnel is absolute torture for him. It is not so much the discomfort, restricted vision or attempts to bark becoming unexpectedly amplified that makes him so miserable; what really distresses Tug is that he cannot clean himself.

The daily ritual of licking, scratching, nibbling, shaking and rolling is fundamental to Tug's sense of wellbeing. Licking is the most important part of the body maintenance process for most animals. It removes dirt, dry skin, loose hair and ecto parasites. It cleans wounds, stimulates essential skin oil production and is an extremely pleasant way of passing the time, when nothing else is happening. It is also, even among domesticated pets, one of the most deeply-rooted instincts of animal survival. In their wild state, an animal's struggle for existence depends on cleanliness. It is vital for them to keep their senses alert; coats or feathers must be clean and quiet and bodies free of scent that may attract predators or alert the predated. The majority of wild animals carry fleas or mites but very few will have soiled skins. They cannot afford the luxury. An animal that neglects itself is almost certainly a sick one.

The toilette of birds, performed at least once a day, is essential for keeping their feathers in perfect condition for flying. Amongst other birds, pheasant, partridge and grouse are great dust-bathers, scratching earth until it is loose or finding a sandy or dusty area in which they can lie to throw the powdery dirt all over their bodies. Wings and feathers are held loosely during this operation to allow the dirt to penetrate to the skin where it clogs the breathing apertures of any attached parasites, which fall off when the birds get up and shake themselves.

The next process is careful preening: rumpled feathers are straightened and loose ones removed. Finally, the feathers are oiled. Hidden among the soft feathers at the base of the tail is an oil gland, which varies in size depending on the species – it reaches maximum size in aquatic birds, whose feathers require plenty of waterproofing. The bird's probing beak or bill releases an oily substance which is carefully smeared over every feather. This keeps feathers supple, provides weatherproofing and also keeps the beak from becoming dry and scaly.

Bats are generally considered by the uninitiated as filthy creatures. Nothing could be further than the truth. Because they live in such closely packed roosts, which inevitably attracts vermin, bats spend up to an hour a day carefully licking and nibbling through their fur to remove mites and fleas. Those parts that cannot be reached with their tongues, such as the ears – which are crucial to their ability to hunt successfully – are cleaned by the curious protuberance in the centre of their wing edges known as the 'thumb'. Particular attention is paid to the delicate wing structure and a portion of time always devoted to massaging the tiny wing 'hands' and feet with their tongues.

Ground animals vulnerable to predators are particularly thorough in their cleanliness. We have all watched rabbits outside their burrows on a sunny day, rigorously washing, and moles, when not tunnelling for worms, endlessly clean themselves, but this is nothing compared to the obsessional fastidiousness of a hare. As a surface dweller, a hare relies for protection entirely on two things – its speed and its ability to disguise any trace of scent. The hare lies up by day in a form commanding a good field of vision, venturing forth to feed at dawn and dusk. Before and after feeding the animal performs a rigorous cleansing routine that would put any cat to shame. Squatting on its haunches, a hare shakes any loose dirt from its pads, before licking each one scrupulously clean. Saliva-moistened forepaws are then used to wash the face, whiskers and ears, which are pushed forward in reach of its tongue. Every inch of the coat is then thoroughly licked clean, with special attention to the genitals.

Horses, cattle and deer 'skin twitch' to remove dirt and irritants from parts of the body that cannot be reached by tongue, teeth or tail. They, and various other mammals including voles, often make the daily clean-up something of a social occasion and groom each other.

All the *mustelidae* – badgers, otters, ferrets, weasels and stoats – have a high standard of hygiene. Otters devote meticulous attention to their coats, particularly if their territory is tidal, carefully removing any vestige of salt and ensuring that the undercoat is in perfect condition to trap air for buoyancy and insulation. All create latrines clear of their habitat and a brock, perhaps the cleanest of them all, regularly changes his bedding.

Foxes, although periodic carrion-eaters, are remarkably dirt free. They may stink, but unless they are sick or old, their coats will be clean and free of parasites. A vixen protects her cubs against vermin by moving them from one earth to another if the first becomes foul.

Curiously enough, it is among insects that cleanliness is raised to an art form. Bees take painstaking care over the maintenance of wings and antennae; ants lick themselves every few minutes with an oily saliva to sanitise and lubricate their bodies. Neither will tolerate the least dirt or debris in their abode. Within the social hierarchy, worker bees are assigned to clean their queen and slave ants, their masters.

Which seems to be my role with Tug these days. He is not a dog who normally encourages familiarity, but with his one good eye glaring balefully from inside the plastic funnel, he just about tolerates his pads being washed and his coat brushed.

Oak Apple Day

May is the month when wild flower growth is at its most stunning, with gorse, meadow vetchling, cowslips, buttercups, celandine, dandelion, bird's-foot trefoil and yellow rattle throwing a golden sheen across heaths, wood margins and meadows. Verges on every country lane gleam white as stitchwort, wild parsley, white dead-nettle and hawthorn come into flower. Woodland floors are carpeted with bluebells, pink purslane, red campion, purple-flowered bittersweet, wood sorrel, blue speedwell and sweet woodruff, in their last flush of growth before the leaf canopy closes over them. A haze of yellow, pink or white blossom surrounds laburnum, ash, horse chestnut, crab apple, rowan, sycamore or white beams and on the great twisted oak which towers over the knowe behind the farmhouse, fragile pale green catkins appear as they have done every May for hundreds of years.

The oak is the national tree of England, representing our strength and endurance, and it saddens me that Oak Apple Day, once an occasion for national rejoicing, is now scarcely recognised as a cause for celebration. The date, 29th May, was the birthday of King Charles II and the day of his triumphant return to London in 1660, marking the restoration of the monarchy and the end of the nine, gloomy, repressive years of Cromwell's Republic, during which almost anything enjoyable had been banned. The populace was understandably ecstatic. Soon afterwards Parliament commanded that this 'Happy Restoration' should forever be observed as a public holiday and day of thanksgiving for redemption from tyranny, marked with church services — a special blessing was included in the Book of Common Prayer — bell ringing, dancing and bonfires. An oak tree was adopted by Charles as his personal badge, to commemorate the day in 1651 when he and his cavalry commander,

William Carless, evaded capture after the battle of Worcester by hiding in an oak tree near Boscabel House in Shropshire. Sprigs of oak leaves, preferably with the oak-apples attached, became symbolic of Royalist support and an integral part of the Oak Apple Day celebrations.

The nation had much to be grateful for; the Merry Monarch was a man of taste, vision and foresight, a patron of the arts, science and the Turf. Cavaliers returning from exile brought back innovative farming ideas which led to the Agricultural Revolution and laid the foundations of Britain's future prosperity. Until the late nineteenth century, churches, civic buildings, houses, carriage and farm horses – even railway engines – were all garlanded with oak boughs, sometimes with the leaves and oak apples gilded. Church bells rang, bonfires sent showers of sparks into the summer night and anyone not sporting a sprig of oak leaves on their lapel or hat was likely to be beaten up or, at the very least, pelted with rotten eggs and manure.

In 1859, Oak Apple Day ceased to be a public holiday, having been abolished under the Anniversary Days Observance Act of that year. The service of blessing was removed from prayer books, the spray of oak leaves, which had long adorned one side of our sixpences and shillings, was replaced with the British lion and the custom gradually went into decline.

Remnants of Oak Apple Day were still active in the 1950s and I remember the occasion as the high point of the summer term at prep school. Known as 'Pinch Bum Day', there was a frantic scramble through the woods in the school grounds on the 28th May to secure sprigs of the protective leaf for the following day. Most sought-after were those with the yellowish, irregular shaped oak apples which provided considerable entertainment on their own. The unsuspecting could be persuaded that they were edible – for though oak apples have little smell, they are incredibly astringent. Also they were quite hard when thrown as well as being the source of endless fascination when dissected, revealing a series of tiny chambers containing miniscule grubs.

An oak apple is actually a gall or abnormal growth in plant tissue caused by the little female gall wasp, *biorhiza pallida*, who lays her eggs in early spring on the leaf bud of an oak tree, usually an English or Common oak. The developing larvae create a chemical reaction with the tree's organism, which produces layers of tissues completely enveloping the larvae and eventually resembling a small apple. Inside, there may be as many as thirty separate chambers containing larvae, which pupate and chew their way out in June or July. The oak apples, which dry out, wither completely and become detached from the tree in autumn. They contain gallotannic acid and were once harvested for dyes and ink, or used medicinally to relieve burns, soothe haemorrhoids and as a gargle for sore throats.

Apart from the solitary Royalist in the Scottish Borders defiantly wearing an oak leaf in his buttonhole on 29th May, few people still observe the historic occasion. In Worcester, the 'Faithful City', the Guildhall is decorated with oak boughs and a pageant is held on the steps, where enthusiasts in period costume are met by the Lord Mayor and civic dignitaries. At Northampton, to which the King gave a thousand tons of oak after the town was virtually destroyed by fire in 1685, a service of thanksgiving is held at the magnificent All Saints Church and the royal effigy above the portico dressed with oak leaves. The Chelsea Pensioners of the Royal Hospital cover the statue of their founder with oak garlands and parade in his honour before a member of the royal family, wearing their scarlet dress uniforms and tricorn hats, before tottering off for their traditional blow-out of beer and plum pud. Nowadays even this deeply emotive ceremony sometimes has to wait until after the Chelsea Flower Show.

Summer

Blind Stinger

Apond on a warm day in June is an enchanting place, a world humming with activity and fecund growth. All one's senses are engaged: one can hear the drone of insects and smell the rich scent of meadow sweet and willow herb; see Red Admirals flitting among the marsh marigold and yellow iris, water boatmen scudding along the surface and perhaps a moorhen and her dusty yellow chicks swimming surreptitiously along the edge of a bed of reed mace; or even a mallard and her flappers, peering cautiously through the burr reeds. As I watch, a splash of a feeding fish draws my eye to the centre of the pond and the flash of iridescent blue as a Hawker dragonfly swoops at a cloud of midges hovering above a lily pad.

I never see one of these glorious insects without hearing a voice from childhood shouting 'run for it, that thing can kill a horse' and, as I scampered for home, an older sister gleefully speeding me on my way with horrifying tales of the 'horse stinger's' capabilities. The three-pronged tail was deadly, from which no living creature was safe. It transported goblins and water witches on its back. It was known as 'the blind stinger' because it ate small boys' eyes and 'the devil's darning needle' from stitching up their lips so that they starved to death. It was only weeks later, whilst earnestly warning the gardener against venturing near the lily pond that I learnt, with a mixture of disappointment and relief, that I had been conned.

The fallacy that dragonflies could sting, let alone carry venom powerful enough to kill a horse, in no way diminished the thrill of interest whenever I saw one. During its short summer life span the male dragonfly is a splendidly aggressive hunter, whose sole aim in life is to satisfy an insatiable appetite and to mate. Both dragonflies and the smaller damselflies belong to the insect order *Odanata*, meaning toothed. There are two types of dragonfly: the stocky Darter that spends most of its time clinging to reeds or other water plants, occasionally leaping out at prey or in pursuit of a partner, and the more active Hawker. These are the ones most commonly seen, restlessly patrolling their territories in a variety of shimmering colours and periodically performing amazing feats of aerobatics. Dragonflies have four gossamer-thin, veined wings, each of which moves independently, enabling them to hover, fly backwards, loop-the-loop or hurtle forward at impressive speed when prey is spotted through their enormous compound eyes.

A dragonfly's appetite covers anything aerial smaller than itself – horseflies, mosquitoes, midges, gnats, flying ants, butterflies, their damselfly relations and other dragonflies who make the mistake of invading the wrong territory. A particularly hungry yellow and black dragonfly was reported to *The Field* magazine in 1957 having seized the fly of a fisherman in the New Forest, releasing it only when it was discovered to be inedible. Victims are grabbed by the two spiny, forward legs and either voraciously eaten on the wing or taken to some handy resting place and dismembered. Mating is performed in flight, the male seizing his partner by the back of the head with feelers at the end of his abdomen. They land on some convenient stalk for the female to create a 'mating wheel' by bringing her genitals up to the sperm capsule on the male's second abdominal segment. The female still held by the head, the courting couple fly off together and remain joined while she inserts her fertilised eggs just below water in plant tissue. Within a day or two, the eggs hatch and another generation begins the longest stage in a dragonfly's life cycle, as a nymph.

In its murky, underwater world, dragonfly larvae are almost more formidable than the adults. Nymphs, which can grow to fifty-five millimetres in size, are ferocious predators of tadpoles, wireworms, blood worms, water beetles and spiders, fresh water shrimps, fish fry and the larvae of other dragonflies. They crawl ponderously among the weeds and vegetable debris watching for available food through huge eyes, perfectly camouflaged by their dingy, dark khaki colouring. Nymphs obtain oxygen from water sucked into their bodies through rectal gills and, when movement of a food source is detected, expelled water propels them forward at astonishing speed. At the same time a prehensile lip, an extension of the lower jaw with spiked pincers at the extremity, known as the mask, shoots out to impale the prey. Once the nymph has eaten, the lip is folded away beneath its chin.

Most species of dragonfly larvae over-winter amongst plant stems and under stones or submerged logs. Some of the larger species, like the Darter larvae, remain nymphs for up to five years, repeatedly shedding their skins. In the spring that they metamorphose, the developing nymph indulges in a last feeding frenzy. It then rests for a day or two, whilst it ceases to breathe through gills and adapts to taking oxygen through spiracles, before clambering up the stalk of a plant and out of water. The hard, leathery skin begins to split and one of nature's most brilliant creatures laboriously emerges, often far larger than the abandoned exuvia. This usually happens at night to avoid predators and allow the wings to take shape and harden. A hatching of young dragonflies in the dawn light is a wonderful sight – a number of dragonflies seen together is known as a 'dazzle'. As the sun comes up, the dragonfly is ready to embark on a new life lasting only a few months.

Both the smaller adults and nymphs are prey to fish, particularly trout, with female dragonflies especially at risk when laying their eggs below the water line. Dragonflies need sunlight for energy and remain immobile on cloudy days. In prolonged bad weather, many die of starvation. When perched, they are vulnerable to other predators too – frogs, toads and lizards and a variety of birds – but on the wing, few British birds can match them for aerial dexterity.

Dragonflies, damselflies, cockroaches and silverfish are the oldest form of insect. They remain unchanged, except in size, since prehistoric times. There are thirty-four species of dragonfly in the UK of which the largest, the beautiful blue Emperor, has a wing span of eleven centimetres. There is one in South America with a span of nineteen centimetres, whilst fossil remains of dragonflies dating back three hundred million years show an insect with a wing span of eighty centimetres. Makes one wonder how big the midges were.

Mallard

One year in the middle of March, a mallard duck made her nest of leaves, twigs and the down from her breast feathers in the bole of an old pollarded hazel on a steep bank above the Liddel Water, not far from the farmhouse. Her eggs took twenty-eight days to hatch and I would sometimes see her during our hill lambing, creeping along the water's edge with her eight ducklings trailing in line behind. In June, they were still too heavy to fly but beginning to 'scutter', using their little under-developed wings and both feet to bounce themselves across the surface of the water. No doubt observation of this comic and frantic effort to fly was how the children's game of ducks and drakes originated.

There are mallard on every park lake, pond and mere, not just in Britain, but worldwide. The name 'mallard' derives from the Latin *masculus* and the Old German *hart*, meaning hardy or bold. Until the middle of the twentieth century the generic term for the species was Wild Duck, with only the green-headed drakes referred to as mallards.

There is nothing more aggressively masculine than the pursuit flight of a drake. As the mating season wears on and fertilised ducks begin nesting, bands of drakes will pursue spare females and try to mate with them by force, without bothering with any form of courtship routine. Mallard rapes involving several drakes and repeated assaults are common in parks where there is overcrowding and nests too close together, and although this is a fairly modern phenomenon, Chaucer, in his poem *The Parlement of Foules*, describes the loutish mallard as a ''stroyer of his owne kind', with language that came out of the dunghill.

I can never look at a mallard drake without thinking about the magnificently dotty and eccentric Mallard Hunt performed by the

Fellows of All Souls College, Oxford, after their Gaudy, or Feast, on 14th January. Founded in 1483 by Henry VI, All Souls has no undergraduates and its Fellows are among the finest academic minds in the world.

Legend has it that when the foundations were being laid, an enormous mallard drake was disturbed, which took flight and evaded capture. Hence, on every Mallard Night, after the feasting had ended, a search was made for the mythical bird by all the Fellows, led by an elected Lord Mallard and six officers bearing white staffs. Sometime after midnight, following a dinner of perhaps fourteen courses and as many vintages, the whole company of Fellows stumbled forth in riotous procession singing the Mallard Song, preceded by a man with a live mallard attached to a long pole. Every hall, room, closet, passage, cellar, attic and even the roofs had to be inspected in a search which required frequent breaks for refreshment and lasted until after dawn.

The origins of this extraordinary custom have been lost in obscurity, but there are suggestions of a connection to the sexual behaviour of mallard drakes, as indicated in the chorus of the song:

> *Oh by the blood of King Edward,*
> *Oh by the blood of King Edward,*
> *it was a swapping, swapping Mallard.*

The Old English meaning of the word 'swap' was to throw down, strike upon, or fix upon something or someone, and, in the spirit of the song, it probably has sexual connotations.

Not everyone was a wholehearted supporter of this ancient tradition. In 1632, George Abbot, Archbishop of Canterbury, who happened to be staying in Oxford on 14th January, wrote peevishly and at length to the Warden of All Souls of the '… great outrage committed in your college… where men did never before break forth into such intolerable liberty as to tear down doors and gates, and disquiet their neighbours as if it had been a camp or town at war'. Another description comes from

Reginald Heber, subsequently Archbishop of Calcutta, who observed forty or fifty people staggering about the roofs of All Souls in the early hours of 15th January 1802, waving lighted torches and remarked that '… all who lived within half a mile must have been awakened by the manner in which they thundered out the Song…'.

After this particularly riotous Mallard Hunt, it was decided the ceremony would cease to be held annually and henceforth become centennial. In 1901, Cosmo Lang, a future Archbishop of Canterbury, was Lord Mallard and apparently sang every verse and chorus of the Mallard Song several times quite beautifully, whilst clinging to the spire of All Souls chapel. At the 2001 Gaudy, one hundred and eighteen Fellows and Quondam Fellows sat down to dinner, amongst them John Redwood and the Hon. William Waldegrave, once members of a Conservative cabinet; and Lord Neill of Bladen, a former chairman of the Committee for Standards in Public Life. For the first time, lady Fellows were also in attendance. Dr Martin West, Emeritus Scholar of All Souls and Kenyon Medallist for Classical Studies, was Lord Mallard, bellowing the Mallard Song in true tradition as he was carried round the college on the shoulders of his elected officers.

It seems sad the Mallard Hunt is now so rarely celebrated, but it does give an insight into something unique about the British psyche. Regardless of whatever else may be happening in the world, there is every expectation that in 2101, the cream of academia, judges, bishops and elder statesmen will stagger forth again after a fourteen-course dinner and enough port to sink a battleship, to perpetuate a tradition started in 1438. I expect the menu has probably already been chosen.

Green Parakeets

In the late 1500s, Dr Johannes Caius, founder of the ancient Cambridge college and physician to three English monarchs, including Queen Elizabeth I, observed that: 'We Englishe men are marvailous greedy gaping gluttons after novelties and covetous cormourantes after things that be seldom, rare, straunge and hard to get.' Since these words were written, our passion for the exotic has led to over a hundred alien species becoming naturalised animals of the British Isles. Some are relatively harmless and have little impact on the indigenous fauna but others like grey squirrels and mink have done immense damage. For the moment, the jury is out on which category should contain the escalating flocks of feral green parakeets roosting in London's leafy suburbs and the surrounding counties.

Rose-ringed or green parakeets are decorative birds, with emerald body plumage, long, pale-blue tails, red beaks and a pink and black ring round their faces and necks. They are great acrobats and one of nature's comics: garrulous, inquisitive, fearless and mischievous. These characteristics, the ease with which they learn to mimic words, coupled with their size – around forty centimetres, of which half is tail feathers – made them one of the most popular aviary pets for several centuries.

They were first recorded in the wild at the Gurney family home, Northrepps Hall in Norfolk, in 1855. It was assumed that these birds were killed off by the series of cold winters in the latter half of that century. Feral green parakeets were subsequently observed in the 1930s, when a number of birds could often be seen roosting in the trees on the edge of Epping Forest and feeding in gardens at Loughton, Woodford and Epping. The failure of these birds to survive in the wild was again attributed to extreme winter temperatures.

In 1969, there was a series of simultaneous sightings of small roosts at Southfleet near Rochester, Gravesend, Shorne, Bromley, Beckenham and Croydon. Over the next five years, green parakeets were regularly seen at Langley Park, Ashtead, Bookham, Chessington, Claygate and Esher. Others were recorded around Dorking, Guildford, Old Windsor, Marlow, Wraybury in Buckinghamshire and Woodford Green across the Thames in Essex.

There was considerable speculation as to where the birds came from, with each area claiming a different provenance. The east side of London claimed they were part of the cargo on a ship that got into difficulty at the mouth of the Thames and were humanely released as the vessel sank. Those in Surbiton believed the birds were escapees from a film set at Shepperton. Then as parakeets began to appear around Slough and Windsor, they were assumed to have eluded customs officials at Heathrow quarantine centre. Possibly the most fanciful theory was that Jimi Hendrix had started the ball rolling when he released the ones he kept in his Chelsea flat, under the chemically-induced impression that he could fly with them. In actuality, the feral population almost certainly became established from homing aviary birds that simply took off into the wild.

By 1983, an estimated one thousand feral green parakeets were roosting in parks round Greater London south of the Thames, enough to qualify as an addition to the official list of British birds as a Class C (established exotic). Until the late 1990s, there was little increase in numbers and green parakeets remained a suburban novelty, greeting commuters with their cheerful early morning shrieks, feeding from bird tables, predating on gardens, performing aerial acrobatics and hanging upside-down from telephone wires. Since then, the population around London has exploded to over ten times that number, with at least half occupying a raucous roost in the Lombardy poplars beside the Esher Rugby Club ground. Nor are they any longer confined to suburban parks and gardens, researchers estimating that there are another ten thousand parakeets across the south-west, West Midlands, Wales and East Anglia.

In 2018, a reputed fifty thousand green parakeets live in the UK – fifteen times more than in 1995, which makes them the fastest growing UK bird species, increasing at a rate of thirty per cent each year. The birds have expanded from the home counties as far north as Inverness and west to Bristol. Inevitably, as roosting space fills up in urban areas, parakeets will become increasingly established near farmland.

Several factors have favoured this escalation in numbers. The natural distribution of green parakeets is across south-east Asia, the damp foothills of the Himalayas and subtropical Africa. This makes them ideally suited to the mild, wet winters we have nowadays, with suburban birds further protected by the ambient temperature from central heating. Their roosts are always in tall deciduous trees – ash, oak, poplars, beech, chestnuts – and they have few predators apart from jays, grey squirrels and peregrines. Cocks and hens become sexually active in their second year, with the hen laying between two and four eggs. Like all the parrot family, they live to a great age, over thirty years in captivity and twenty in the wild. As vegetarians, there is no shortage of food, with flocks dispersing noisily from their roosts at daylight and travelling considerable distances in search of buds, berries, all soft fruit, nuts and grain.

As increasing numbers of parakeets spread across rural areas, there is growing concern among arable farmers and fruit growers at the inevitable impact on production by crop predation. Parakeets are notorious for the damage large flocks cause each year in south-east Asia and India, where fruit trees and grain fields are stripped in a matter of hours. There are already cases of orchards, soft fruit farms and vineyards in Kent, Surrey and Berkshire being attacked by companies of parakeets swooping in from their roosts in the London suburbs. The scale of damage is marginal and localised at the moment, but will soar as figures reach the hundred thousand.

There is equal apprehension by ornithologists at the effect the escalating green parakeet population must have on our indigenous bird life. Green parakeets are hole-nesters, relying on existing cavities in buildings, in trees and the nests of others, rather than making their own. They mate earlier than our own cavity-nesters, reducing breeding sites for woodpeckers, kestrels, little owls (themselves an alien species introduced from Italy in 1870) and starlings. Furthermore, competition for food, their aggressive behaviour and loud, incessant squawking is likely to drive away less robust indigenous and rare migratory woodland birds.

Britain's green parakeet population seems destined to become yet another destructive alien pest species and controlling them, an immensely costly operation. Given the precedence of lost opportunities in the history of introduced exotics, government inertia seems inexcusable. There is much wisdom in the old adage 'an ounce of prevention is worth a pound of cure'.

Luck

Throughout one muggy day in June, I had feathered the water of a little trout stream which tumbles down off Dartmoor without a hint of a pull. Normally it was a trout fisherman's paradise, with deep secret pools, shaded by oak, ash and sycamore, where kingfishers dart and brilliant dragonflies hover; gravelly runs and stickles, open glides and fast shallows; but not one of these features seemed to help on that oppressively warm, early summer day. Several times I retired to the bank and sat amongst the wild garlic, pink campion and cow parsley to study the flies in my old aluminium fly box. I changed the Blue Winged Olive for a Black Gnat, or the Pheasant Tail Nymph for a Hares Ear, more in hope than expectation.

The atmospheric pressure dropped in the afternoon and the midges became unbearable, gathering in clouds under the overhang, wriggling into my eyebrows and savaging my wrists at the shirt cuff. I was reeling in with the intention of packing up for the day, when an observation of Ovid's came unbidden to my mind: 'Luck affects everything; let your hook always be cast; in the stream where you least expect it, there will be a fish.' With June being such an exceptionally warm month, I had been fishing the faster water on the basis that fish would have moved up into more oxygenated areas: but irritated by Ovid into a final cast, I flicked my fly across a deep pool, dropping it beneath the overhang of a bank, where I was pretty certain there wouldn't be a fish. Working the fly across I was amazed to feel the line suddenly tighten and see the tip of my rod dip; the midges were forgotten as I had a blissful tussle for the next quarter of an hour, eventually landing a very decent little brownie.

At the hotel, my triumph was greeted by others in the fishing party driven back by disappointment and the midges, as pure luck – but was it? Luck and the different interpretations of those well-worn words such as chance, probability, self-fulfilling prophecy, fortune, divine providence, fate, serendipity and meaningful coincidences, became the topic of a conversation that dominated the evening.

Each of us knew someone who had cruised insouciantly through life: lucky in birth, cupped and capped at school and university, lucky in love, lucky in their marriage, lucky at cards, horses, investments and even, in one instance, lucky with the Lotto. Equally we all knew unfortunates whose lives were dogged by unremitting misfortune, with calamity following calamity in dark and dreary procession. Various friends and acquaintances had experienced miraculous escapes from disaster, accident or disease. Conversely, of course, we also knew some who by evil luck were in the wrong place at the wrong time and became victims of some ghastly tragedy.

As the evening wore on and the decanter did its rounds, someone recalled reading Professor Robert Merton's thesis on self-fulfilling prophecies (a term he coined in 1948) and the discussion soared to an intellectual level which, mercifully, no one could remember much about at breakfast the following morning.

The definition of luck varies by the cultural, emotional, philosophical, religious or mystical perspective of the person interpreting it and is described in Webster's dictionary as 'a purposeful, unpredictable and uncontrollable force that shapes events favourably or unfavourably for an individual, group or cause'. The people of early civilisations, riven by superstition and with multiple deities influencing every aspect of their lives, each had their god or goddess of luck. The Ancient Egyptian had the snake god, Agathadaemon, and the Greeks, Tyche, the blind mistress of fortune, whose temple in Alexandria was the most magnificent of the entire Hellenic world. The Romans adopted Tyche and turned her into Fortuna, the goddess of fate and fortune, personifying good or bad luck in Roman religion and representing life's capriciousness. The goddess was multifaceted, with at least twenty different aspects ranging from

Fortuna Annonaria, the luck of the harvest, and Fortuna Muliebris, the luck of a woman in marriage, to Fortuna Redux, the luck which brought one safely home from a journey and Fortuna Publica Populi Romani, the official collective good luck of the Roman people. The date of 11th June was sacred to the goddess but each of the facets had its own festival throughout the year, with her own festival on 24th June being the most important.

Temples to Fortuna proliferated all over the empire, of which the temple of Fortuna Primigena – the luck of the firstborn – in Praeneste, was undoubtedly the largest. An immense edifice, it was visible for miles, occupying five vast terraces, which were built on gigantic masonry substructures connected by elaborate grand staircases. These rose up on the hillside in the form of a pyramid with the round temple of Fortuna crowning the uppermost terrace.

The name seems to have derived from *Vortumna*, which loosely translates as 'she who revolves the year'. It is this analogy that led to the belief in the Wheel of Fortune, itself emblematic of the uncertainty of life, the sudden transformation from prosperity to disaster – or vice versa – thus illustrating fortune's capricious nature.

The earliest written reference to the Wheel of Fortune is to be found in Seneca's tragedy *Agamemnon*, written in 55 BC:

> *Whatever Fortune has raised on high, she lifts but to bring low.*
> *Modest estate has longer life; then happy he whoe'er, content with*
> *the common lot, with safe breeze hugs the shore, and, fearing to*
> *trust his skiff to the wider sea, with unambitious oar keeps close to*
> *land.*

Equally descriptive was Ovid's rueful observation after he had been exiled by the Emperor Augustus to Tomis, now Constanta in Romania, writing gloomily:

The goddess who admits by her unsteady wheel her own fickleness;
she always has its apex beneath her swaying foot.

The early Christian church found it expedient to tolerate the concept of Fortuna, cleverly interpreting the random and sometimes catastrophic turns of Fortune's Wheel as part of God's hidden purpose. Fortuna became a servant of God and the good or bad events that affected people individually or collectively were all part of Divine Will. Her sacred day and personal festival, 11th and 24th June, were replaced by St Barnabas' Day and St John's Day, both significant events in the Christian calendar.

Despite the best efforts of the church, good luck charms, a largely pagan belief, remained as popular as they had been for millennia and virtually everyone carried one, whether this was a hare's foot, a hag stone (a stone with a hole through the middle), the little T-bone from a sheep's skull, or even a dried acorn.

A number of the great families in the north of England and Scotland possessed rare objects, passed from generation to generation and known as 'lucks', upon which the prosperity of the family depended. For example, the Musgraves of Edenhall, near Penrith in Cumbria, had the so-called Luck of Edenhall, an exquisite gilded glass beaker of Middle Eastern origin, decorated with blue, red, green and white enamelling. This had been in the family since the early fifteenth century and is now preserved in the Victoria and Albert Museum. Legend has it that a party of fairies had brought the beaker with them to drink the waters of St Cuthbert's Well close to the Hall but were frightened away, shouting as they abandoned the beaker, 'If this cup should break or fall: Farewell the Luck of Edenhall'.

Of far greater antiquity is the Colstoun Pear, the property of the ancient family of Broun of Colstoun in Haddingtonshire, East Lothian. In the thirteenth century, Sir David Le Brun married the daughter of Sir Hugh de Gifford, Baron of neighbouring Yester, a fairly sinister individual reputed to have necromantic powers. Sir Hugh gave his daughter a fresh pear as her dowry, informing her that as long as the pear was preserved, good fortune would never desert her or her descendants, but if harm should come to it, misfortune would swiftly follow. The pear was encased in a silver casket and the palladium remained intact until the late seventeenth century, when the second Baronet, Sir George Broun, married Lady Elizabeth McKenzie, the daughter of the Earl of Cromartie. She, on being shown the family treasure, succumbed to temptation and took a bite out of it. Disaster immediately struck: the marriage was without issue, Sir George's finances collapsed and he was forced to sell Colstoun to his brother, who was subsequently drowned with his two sons when the coach they were travelling in overturned whilst crossing a swollen river. As the estates and the baronetcy passed to distant cousins, the curse appears to have become lifted and the shrivelled fruit, complete with tooth-marks, is still in its silver casket at Colstoun.

Is it pure luck when a wildfowler stays a little longer when others are packing up and bags the only goose of the morning? Or when the rod who follows Ovid's advice surprises himself and everyone else with a catch? Or do we have an element of influence over events that appear to be beyond our control? The ancients differentiated between luck, chance and fate and, as early as 160 BC, the Roman playwright, Publius Terentius Afer, observed that fortune favoured the bold. It was Seneca who made the profound statement that luck occurred when preparation met opportunity.

In the 1990s, the psychologist Professor Richard Wiseman conducted a ten-year research project into why some people are luckier than others, reaching a variety of conclusions based on his subjects' different personalities. He suggested that unlucky people tended to lack self-confidence, be indecisive and more tense, and that anxiety disrupted their ability to notice the unexpected and to follow intuition when making a choice. Lucky people, on the other hand, seem to be generally assertive, optimistic, relaxed and easy-going, naturally creating or noticing chance opportunities; they then make 'lucky' decisions by following their intuition, create self-fulfilling prophecies through positive expectations and adopt a positive attitude to ill fortune, which often transforms bad luck into good.

In other words, to quote Ernest Hemingway, 'you make your own luck'. *Bonne chance à tous*!

The Heron

On July mornings, when sunrise is at 5.30am and we are away early to work on sheep before the heat of the day, I often see a heron gliding in to take up position in the shallows beside a small pool formed at the confluence of the Liddel and Hermitage waters. Here he stands, one-legged, apparently dozing, eyes half-closed and head sunk between his shoulders, but it takes only the tiniest movement of parr to galvanise the bird's lightning reflexes and the sharp, deadly, pick-axe beak to strike. So successful are herons at catching all manner of fish, from eels to sticklebacks, that at one time their fat was highly prized as bait by anglers, who believed that the birds exuded oil from their legs and feet which was irresistible to fish.

Later in the day, when the sun moves round, I may see the heron in the adjoining marshland, stealthily hunting for the fledglings of waterfowl, frogs, newts, water rats, mice, voles, shrews or any of the other small mammals that make up a heron's diet. Acute hearing, remarkable eyesight, silk soft plumage, endless patience and a voracious appetite enable these birds, which appear so ungainly, to be deadly hunters of still or running water, of marsh, pool and ornamental pond.

For much of the year, herons are solitary birds, commuting considerable distances between their feeding and resting grounds with slow, heavy wing beats, their long necks doubled back and legs trailing. In the breeding season, usually between February and May but sometimes running into June, they congregate in communal heronries constructed in tall deciduous trees. They return to the same site year after year, refurbishing the large sprawling nests of twigs and grass or sedges as necessary. Some heronries are enormous, such as the one at Northward Hill overlooking the Thames Marshes near Hoo in Kent, which has over a hundred pairs. Trentham Estate, near Stoke-on-Trent, and Hilgay, near Downham Market on the edge of the Norfolk Fens, each have around fifty.

A heronry at breeding time is fascinating to watch; courtship and nest building is preceded by elaborate dancing, posturing, neck weaving, wing beating and beak snapping. The hen lays between three and five light blue eggs, which are incubated by both parents and hatch after about twenty-five days. The young are fed by each adult bird in turn, and leave the heronry after a couple of months. The noise from even a small heronry of half a dozen pairs has to be heard to be believed, whilst the racket from a big one is deafening. From the moment the mating season starts until the last of the young have left, there is a continual cacophony of hoarse, raucous barks, squawks and honks from dawn 'til dusk, as the adults squabble over nesting areas and the young perpetually shriek for food. The appalling smell from bird dung and the detritus of food scraps under the heronry is never to be forgotten and this, coupled with the din and sight of these great birds swooping in as the light fades, is an eerily prehistoric experience.

Herons use their six-foot wing span, twice the length of their bodies, to gain altitude very rapidly; it was this capacity to soar when pursued that once made herons the falconer's ultimate quarry. Heron hawking was so highly prized in early medieval Europe that herons were considered the property of the Crown and, after the Norman Conquest, English heronries were listed in the Domesday Book. The oldest surviving one is in a stand of beeches beside the Pilgrims' Way near Chilham Castle in Kent, on a bluff overlooking the Stour Valley, where the weary pilgrims would have caught their first sight of the spire and towers of Canterbury Cathedral. Once one of England's largest heronries, the number of pairs has dropped from a hundred in 1913 to a mere handful today, despite good stocks of fish in the castle lake and the nearby Stour. This is an alarming situation for the castle's owners: for legend has it that disaster will befall them if no herons are nesting on St Valentine's Day.

The spectacle provided by heron hawking was unsurpassed and to possess a well-stocked heronry in open country was every noble's ambition. Falconers positioned themselves downwind of a heronry, waiting for a bird returning in the afternoon. A cast of (two) long-winged hawks – peregrines or gyrfalcons – were flown and when the heron realised his danger, he disgorged his food and climbed frantically, with the falcons spiralling after him. The first hawk stooped as soon as he was above the heron, forcing him to side-slip, giving the second hawk the opportunity to stoop. In what was considered a good flight, this would be repeated several times with all three birds rising to a great height, until both hawks seize or 'bind' to the heron and slowly descend to the ground.

For many centuries, herons were protected for falconry by an Act of Parliament and although virtually inedible, their status as quarry elevated them to being served at ceremonial feasts in the company of exotics such as swans or peacocks. Protection lapsed during Cromwell's Commonwealth, when falconry was seen as a Royalist pastime. There was a revival of enthusiasm for hawking in the nineteenth century, but by then marshland reclamations had taken much of the heron's habitat and the population had declined, with many of the great heronries being abandoned.

Herons became a protected species again in 1981 under the Wildlife and Countryside Act and there are now around fourteen thousand breeding pairs.

The Shepherd's Dog

A Shepherd's Dog is a delightful essay in *The Shepherd's Calendar* by James Hogg, the Ettrick Shepherd (1770-1835), in which he wrote:

A single shepherd and his dog will accomplish more in gathering a stock of sheep from a highland farm than twenty shepherds could without dogs, and it is a fact that without this docile animal the pastoral life would be blank. Without the shepherd's dog, the whole of the mountainous land in Scotland would not be worth sixpence.

This was written at the end of the eighteenth century during the main thrust of the Enclosure Acts, when vast flocks of sheep were being established on the open heaths and moorlands of northern England and Scotland. Fifty years later, as grouse moors and driven shooting developed, he might have included the sportsman's gundog as an equally vital component of the viability of the uplands. Such observations are as valid today as they were one hundred and fifty years ago: without the sportsman's gundog, there could be no shooting industry and without the shepherd's dog, Britain's population of thirty-five million sheep could not exist.

Our modern gundogs – retrievers, pointers and setters – evolved at the same time as the border collie, the most famous sheepdog in the world. Both were influenced by the same dramatic changes to the British countryside which started at the beginning of the eighteenth century.

Graham Markham, in *Hunger's Prevention or the Whole Art of Fowling by Water and Land* (1655), and Nicholas Cox, in the fourth edition of a *Gentleman's Recreations* (1697), refer to the only 'gun' or 'fowling' dogs being a variety of types loosely termed as spaniels, valued for their intelligence, nose and retrieving qualities.

Rough-coated water spaniels were the most numerous, since the majority of available winged game was on the marshes and wetlands, but on land there were two sorts: crouching and springing. Crouching spaniels included setting dogs: these quartered ground and held birds immobile, whilst either a net was drawn over them or a shot could be loosed off from the immensely cumbersome shotguns of the period. The second crouching type were designated pipers: small, active dogs, used by the decoy men who operated the purpose-built commercial duck decoys to lure large numbers of wildfowl down the pipe of the decoy to the nets at the far end. Springing spaniels, and the smaller cocking spaniels, had originally been bred to 'spring' game to falcons or greyhounds and were still used to flush birds into static nets.

Sheepdogs, on the other hand, came in all shapes and sizes and were the same rough-coated, general purpose droving dogs which had been in existence since domesticated sheep were introduced by the Bronze Age people in 2000 BC.

The agricultural improvements started during the Restoration were intensified and fuelled by the demand created by several factors. These included rapidly expanding colonisation, an Act of Parliament in 1690 'for encouraging the distilling of spirits from corn', a large standing army and a rising population, all of which led to a massive expansion in grain production and great changes to the landscape. As common land was enclosed for arable farming, the first of what eventually became two hundred thousand miles of hedgerows appeared, providing both food and cover for a variety of quarry species and partridges in particular.

The popularity of shooting gathered momentum and sporting guns, although still with immensely long barrels, became lighter and more manageable.

After the Treaty of Utrecht in 1713, officers returning from the continental wars introduced Spanish pointers, which now joined setting dogs in finding and holding birds. The water spaniel remained the dog of choice for the wildfowler.

By the middle of the century, the continuing need for agricultural expansion led to a new series of Parliamentary Enclosure Acts, which were to occur almost annually for the next hundred years. During this period approximately three million hectares of common land were enclosed. As traditional lowland sheep walks were ploughed out for arable production, graziers began to establish sheep on the recently enclosed moorlands and heaths of northern England and southern Scotland and later, once the red deer had been ruthlessly culled, in the Highlands. Graziers who rented hill land first had to clear it of scrub and old rank heather by slashing and burning to improve the natural herbage and then establish sheep over vast areas of ground that was impossible to fence because of the topography and risk of sheep being trapped by snow in winter.

The shepherd's dog had to adjust to the new environment and it is a reflection of the extraordinary ability of dogs to adapt to man's needs, that instead of working close at hand and driving sheep as they had for centuries, they now learnt to work at a distance and develop wide outruns to gather sheep off high ground.

The existing shepherds' dogs at the time all had one characteristic in common: as with their direct descendant, the bearded collie of today, they moved sheep by barking and their bouncing, energetic body action. Shepherds soon found that these dogs were too forceful, both for the complex business of training specific numbers of timid hill sheep to graze only certain areas of hill, and in moving ewes and lambs long distances over rough ground to handling pens.

Border collies, however, move sheep by silent, implied threat, employing rapid, sinuous, crouching movements and, above all, 'eye'

– fixing the sheep, or a sheep, with an inflexible, fixed gaze, resonating power, from which they will naturally turn and run as they are unable to face it. It is these qualities, combined with abnormally high intelligence and an overwhelming desire to please their handler, which make the border collie so superb at herding sheep and led to the breed being the backbone of the sheep industry in Australia, New Zealand, Canada and North and South America.

Where then did the early hill men find these characteristics and transform the working dog? There are, of course, no records, but burning heather for grazing led to an increase in the grouse population; by 1780, British gunmakers were producing improved, shorter barrelled shotguns and lairds were beginning to walk up grouse over setting dogs. One day, somewhere out on the moors, unnoticed whilst a laird and his shepherd were deep in conversation, the same genes that were to become part of the English, Gordon and Irish setter were passed to the sheepdog and eventually became the distinguishing feature of both breeds.

All dogs, to a greater or lesser extent, regard their master as a 'pack leader' and endeavour to please by bringing things to him. Retrievers are an obvious example but this trait is particularly highly developed in the collie and visible at a very young age. We have free-range chickens running about the steading and soon after weaning, a collie pup will spend hours gathering them together and 'wearing' them to the back door of the farmhouse. Once a young dog has been taught discipline and has grown in strength and pace, this natural gathering instinct is developed and expanded by his handler, first on a few sheep in a field and later, out on the hill in the company of an older dog. Collies are biddable, sensitive, generous animals and training is a long process, but they are very quick to learn and with care, a year-old dog should have style, pace, a strong eye, a bold wide outrun, be steady at lifting sheep, receptive to voice and whistle, and focused on his work. From here, more complicated and intricate disciplines may be taught, such as shedding one or two sheep out of a mob; wearing these away from the others; stopping a sheep indicated by the handler, penning sheep and the hardest of the lot, since it is contrary to their gathering instinct, driving sheep away from their handler.

The rationalisation of the old restrictive Game laws in 1830 led to a massive increase in the popularity of shooting and by the second half of the century, shotguns were opening at the breech, driven partridge, pheasant and grouse were becoming all the rage and the railways enabled selective breeding among gundogs. Pointers, the various breeds of setters and spaniels were all now standardised, as were flat, golden, curly-coated and labrador retrievers.

This was the era when practically anything that moved was bet on and field trialling grew out of informal matches when landowners shot together, with the first official trial in 1865, organised by Dr John Henry Walsh, editor of *The Field*. Trialling became immensely popular and the increasing number of meetings held across the country led to the necessity of forming a governing body to ratify the rules and in 1873 the Kennel Club was founded, implementing standards that were to become adopted worldwide.

In the same year, the first sheepdog trial was held at Bala in south Wales. There are now about four hundred trials in the UK alone, ranging from nursery level to the Supreme International Championships at which England, Scotland, Wales and Ireland each enter a team of fifteen dogs.

A trained sheepdog in action is beautiful to watch and I consider myself privileged to have spent my farming life working with a succession of wonderful examples. Apart from the daily routine of moving sheep from high ground in the morning and back in the afternoon, hill collies must adapt throughout the year to changes in temperature, herbage growth and the breeding progress of the flock.

On occasions, they have to adjust to circumstances far beyond their range of experience. Some years ago, I took a little hill collie who had never left home down to London and drove a flock of sheep over London Bridge for a BBC film crew – not once, but several times. The drive itself was to take place at 6am on the pedestrian walkway with the early morning traffic thundering by on my right, whilst on my left, the turgid waters of the Thames slithered past far below. The radio system between the producer and a cameraman mounted on a tall building in Lower Thames Street broke down, reducing the director to hysterics; my co-presenter threw one of her notoriously vocal tantrums and the small, elderly Southdown sheep I had requested turned out to be big, half-bred ewes, recently separated from their lambs and bent on mischief.

The whole thing looked to me like a recipe for disaster, with the likelihood of sheep getting loose all over London, but Nell was completely unfazed by her strange surroundings, by the traffic or the strident voices raised in anger. She crept forward like a cat to move the animals and darted in front to hold them whenever they got too fast. She accomplished her task with apparent ease and we successfully completed the filming.

Wild Goats

There are sheep in every field on either side of the B6399, a single track road that meanders along the Hermitage Water between Newcastleton and Hawick. In one of them, just before the turn-off to the Hermitage Castle, you will invariably see what appears to be a hairy, black hearthrug in a corner where a stone dyke separates the adjacent moorland from the in-bye fields. If you hoot your horn, as I always do, the hearthrug throws up its head, pirouettes on its hind legs, leaps the dyke and gallops off across the moor. I know from experience that it will stop at the top of any high ground and look back in my direction. When it does, I hoot the horn again and it tears off to the top of the next hill, until eventually it disappears over Thiefsike Head, into Raegill Bogs where it belongs. The hearthrug that provides this childish entertainment is a feral goat that was found as a kid, abandoned and starving, out on the moor. The tiny creature, with its satyr's face and disproportionately large ears, was brought home, hand-reared and then when old enough turned loose, to find its kith and kin. Having had a taste of the good life, the goat creeps warily back every day but is off at the first unfamiliar sound.

A fluctuating population of around four thousand feral goats, living in isolated tribes, are scattered across the uplands of Britain. Most are on either side of the Border, the Highlands and Islands, Cumberland, North Wales and on Exmoor. They tend to inhabit remote coastal areas or high rocky ground above the peat line that has plenty of natural shelter.

Wild goats are generally smaller and stockier than domestic breeds, with long curved horns and shaggy, greasy coats which vary in colour from black, red, piebald, skewbald and grey, to pure white. Skins of wild white goats were once in demand for regimental drummer's aprons, whilst the buck's long beards or tassles were used to decorate sporrans of certain Highland regiments.

Timid and suspicious of humans, the goats live in small, matriarchal trips (as they are called) for most of the year, with bucks in separate, hierarchical bachelor units. During the rut, from September until late October, mature bucks gather harems of does together and defend them furiously against other suitors. The goats are particularly annoying on deer forests at this time of year; unlike sheep, which flock together if disturbed, feral goats scatter, making high-pitched snorts of alarm, effectively clearing off any deer within a mile of them. The gestation period is shorter than other livestock and kids – twins are not unusual – are born in January and February. They are hidden for the first few days to protect them from predators and if the weather is hard or the doe is in poor condition, one is invariably abandoned.

All wild goats are descendants of those that were once domesticated. Some tribes may only have been feral for little more than a hundred years, others for many centuries. The important role of goats in the history of British farming has largely been forgotten, but such was their stature in the Middle Ages that Richard II felt moved to present the Bagots, of Blithfield Hall in Staffordshire, with a tribe of goats to thank them for a memorable day's hunting on their estate. This ancient family subsequently adopted a goat's head as their armorial crest. Virtually everyone kept goats, from the nobleman in his castle to the serf in his hut. Hardy and maintenance free, they could be turned away to browse on rough pasture, clearing brambles and weeds, harmful to other livestock, such as buttercups, bracken and ragwort. Until well into the nineteenth century, farmers believed the presence of goats on the same grazing as sheep or cattle was guaranteed to prevent spontaneous abortion.

Goats breed early and kids fatten quickly; in the days when fresh food was strictly governed by the seasons, kid was the first available fresh meat. The milk is easily digestible and, before cows became our main milk source, milking does were kept in every town and village. A doe's ability to produce milk under almost any condition meant they were commonly included on long sea voyages, forming the nucleus of feral tribes in Hawaii, New Zealand and Australia. Meat from pasture-fed goats was more highly prized than mutton and often made into hams; their skins produced parchment and fine 'morocco' leather for shoes and gloves; the long, silky hair was used in wig-making and for high quality ropes.

As a general purpose utility animal, goats were universally kept by crofters and many of the wild goats in the Highlands and Islands are assumed to be descendants of those abandoned during the clearances. Others, such as the feral goats on the Great Orme, near Llandudno in North Wales, stem from escaped park animals, whilst the tribe on Snowdonia are descendants of ancient, semi-domesticated stock kept by Bronze Age pastoralists.

The ones I see sometimes, hunting with the Border Foxhounds high in the Cheviots, are thought to date from the great monastic sheep granges of the early middle ages. The Cistercian monks from Jedburgh, Kelso, Melrose and Dryburgh abbeys, and the Benedictines from the priory on Holy Island, grazed huge flocks of sheep on the Cheviot hills. Goats were always run with these flocks in the belief that they would forage on higher, steeper ground, preventing sheep from straying into places of danger and keeping them on the better grazing of the lower slopes. There is probably some substance to this; goats prefer the more varied diet provided by poorer vegetation and their urine is so pungent that no sheep willingly feeds immediately behind them.

The goats became feral after the Dissolution of the Monasteries and over the centuries, small tribes have survived in the remotest areas of the southern uplands and north Northumberland.

It is hardly surprising that these elusive creatures have chosen to live in the most inaccessible places or that there are so few of them. Given the opportunity, feral goats can be enormously destructive and are notorious tree barkers, particularly in winter, killing young trees and affecting regeneration. As a result, for much of their history every man's hand has been against them. They were persecuted during the eighteenth century when woodland was intensively managed for charcoal, building materials and tanbark. In the early part of the twentieth century, numbers crept back up until there were about two hundred and fifty known wild goat locations but these rapidly diminished due to culling, as post-war soft wood plantations were established in upland districts.

There are thought to be fewer than fifty tribes left now but the population of some of these has increased as a consequence of our milder winters. Goats in the Valley of the Rocks, near Lynton in Devon, have started helping themselves to the flowers in local residents' gardens and the same thing is happening at Nantgwynant in the Snowdonia National Park. Emotions are running high in both places: some people cry 'bring in marksmen', others, 'leave 'em alone'.

Far be it from me to interfere, but has anyone tried hooting their car horn?

Hedging

Of all our deciduous trees, oak, ash, beech, hazel, willow, birch and so on, none are so populous as blackthorn and its cousin, hawthorn. Both grow wild on heaths, scrub farmland, moorland fringes and woodland edges, either as densely branched individual trees of great age, or impenetrable thickets, but their key role in the landscape is as one of the principal species in the living history of our hedgerows.

Hedges are the defining characteristic of lowland Britain and have been used to protect crops and enclose livestock since Neolithic hunter-gatherers established semi-permanent settlements about four thousand years ago, making 'dead' hedges of blackthorn and hawthorn branches. Archaeologists have identified traces of a blackthorn, hawthorn, field maple and buckthorn hedge at Alcester in Warwickshire, carbon-dated to the Iron Age; and excavations at Harmoor in Oxfordshire revealed Roman hedges made from thorn.

The Anglo-Saxons were great hedge planters. The word hedge comes from the Saxon *haeg* and hawthorn from *hagathorn*, with many ancient parish boundaries following the line of Saxon hedges. Our oldest surviving hedge is the 943-year-old Judith's Hedge near Monks' Wood in the parish of Sawtry Judith, Huntingdonshire, planted as a boundary fence in 1075 by Judith of Lens on land given by her uncle, William the Conqueror.

Systematic hedging started in the thirteenth century with the Statute of Merton, which gave lords of the manor the right to enclose common land. Periodic enclosures followed throughout the Middle Ages, with a considerable increase during Tudor times to create sheep pastures. Wool was the backbone of the economy and of enormous benefit to the landowning elite, wool merchants and the Crown, for whom it raised enormous sums. The primary areas of enclosure were in a broad band running from Yorkshire diagonally across England to the south, taking in parts of Norfolk, Suffolk and Cambridgeshire. This led to massive rural depopulation and great hardship – in Leicestershire alone, over thirty villages were abandoned.

The countryside swarmed with starving, dispossessed families and the social unrest eventually led to Kett's Rebellion of 1549; hawthorn acquired the nickname 'Beggars' Bush', from the number of vagrants seeking shelter from the weather beneath the dense, interlocking branches. Despite fears of further agrarian revolt, the need to feed an ever growing population led to well over five thousand individual Enclosure Acts being passed through Parliament from 1604 until 1914, enclosing seven million acres of land, much of it common, waste and heath.

The main thrust of the enclosures took place between 1750 and 1850, when an estimated two hundred thousand miles of hedging was planted, dramatically altering the landscape of lowland Britain and revolutionising fox hunting, particularly in Leicestershire. The rolling countryside and succession of hedges created the historically famous and exhilarating hunting 'black runs', such as the Quorn's Hose Thorns or the Belvoir's Walton Thorns. A whole industry sprang up sourcing and supplying hedging plants and of all the species in the wagons that trundled across the country every autumn – field maple, spindle, hazel, oak, elder, guilder rose, crab apple, holly, dogwood, ash and birch – by far the most important were nature's barbed wire, blackthorn and hawthorn.

Both are related to the Rosaceae family of plants, which includes plums, cherries, apples and roses. Through the winter, the two look very similar to the untutored eye: but blackthorn, *Prunus spinosa*, has a darker bark than hawthorn (hence the name) and in the wild, where hawthorn can grow to ten metres, blackthorn rarely exceeds four. The most obvious difference, though, can be seen in early March, when a 'false spring' in February is followed by a bitter wind blowing from the north-east and our hedgerows and heaths suddenly foam with tiny white flowers as the blackthorn blossoms.

To the ancients, a 'blackthorn winter', with its promise of warm weather to come, was one of nature's most impressive miracles, made all the more remarkable because, unlike other plants, the flowers appear before the leaves. The 'snag bush' blooms as long as the hungry east wind lasts, providing nectar for insects such as bumblebees, hardy enough to brave the cold until the wind changes to the west and the rain which inevitably follows destroys the fragile petals.

The thickets of tangled, interlocking branches are a favourite safe nesting habitat for a variety of small birds and as the temperature warms, blackthorn foliage provides food for an astonishing variety of moth caterpillars. Among them are willow beauty, white-pinion spotted, common emerald, pale November, mottled and green pug, feathered thorn, double square-spot and, occasionally, the brilliant emerald and black hooped caterpillar of the spectacularly beautiful emperor moth.

In June, small green berries emerge, gradually turning into bitter, astringent, inky-skinned fruit in September. Sloes are traditionally harvested when they become more palatable after they have been bletted by the first frosts in October or November, a ripening process which can be achieved nowadays by picking them earlier and putting them in the deep freeze.

At one time, sloes were buried in straw-lined pits for a few months to blet them, a practice which appears to date from Neolithic times, judging by the volume of sloe stones buried at the Stone Age lake village near Glastonbury, and subsequently discovered by archaeologists.

Most sloes are picked to make sloe gin, the all essential mid-morning reviver on a shooting day, but the ancestor of our domestic plum is a versatile and much underrated fruit. Sloes can be made into jams, chutneys, sorbets, tarts and a jelly to accompany venison and lamb, which is vastly superior to redcurrant. They can also be made into a delicious, rich wine similar to port; in the nineteenth century, during the heyday of port consumption, gallons of sloe wine were sold by fraudulent wine merchants as genuine port. Culpeper lists a variety of curative properties for the leaves, flowers, bark and fruit, ranging from fevers, constipation and loose teeth, to intestinal worms and conjunctivitis.

Blackthorn wood is immensely tough and was used to make threshing flails, the teeth of rakes, tool handles and of course, shillelaghs, the Irish fighting cudgel – 'cured' by burying them in a dunghill or smearing them with butter and hanging them in a chimney. A straight blackthorn is much prized by stick dressers; blackthorns are traditionally carried by officers of the Royal Irish Regiment; and each incoming mayor in Sandwich, Kent, is presented with a blackthorn as his badge of office. Ink has been made from the bark and a red dye from the fruit, whilst the long vicious thorns, which make picking sloes a torment, are so hard they were once used as awls.

Folklore comes down heavily in favour of blackthorn as being a malign plant, particularly associated with witches. They are frequently portrayed with a crooked blackthorn staff with which they direct their powers of 'binding and blasting', whilst using the thorns to puncture effigies of those they wished to curse. Blackthorn burns with intense heat and witches were customarily burnt on pyres of blackthorn faggots.

One of the last to meet this fate was Major Thomas Weir of the West Bow in Edinburgh, a Calvinist zealot and signatory to the Solemn League of Covenant. As a preacher, the 'Bowhead Saint' was much admired for the vehemence of his oratory and the manner in which he brandished his carved blackthorn stick to emphasise a point. In 1670, he astounded his congregation by confessing to being a disciple of the devil, a practising witch and also to having an incestuous relationship with his elderly sister, Jean. Initially no one believed him, but when Jean insisted it was all true and that Weir was governed by the evil spirit inhabiting his blackthorn, the Lords Provost had heard enough and condemned them both to death. Jean was hanged on the Grassmarket gallows, whilst Weir and the offending blackthorn were burnt at Leith. His ghost is said to haunt the West Bow, with his spectral blackthorn prancing ahead of him.

Until the Gregorian calendar was introduced in 1752, hawthorn burst into blossom as soon as the blackthorn flowers fell at the end of April. The tiny white or pale pink flowers, after which the Pilgrim Fathers named their ship, had been used as garlands to applaud the start of summer, since the Celts celebrated Beltane, the most important of their four seasonal festivals.

Hawthorn, *Crataegus oxyacantha* is known by various colloquial names: May tree from the flower, making it the only British plant named after the month in which it blooms; whitethorn, from the paleness of its bark compared to blackthorn; and quickthorn, because it is a quick or living hedge, as opposed to a dry or dead one.

As a hedging plant, an individual woodland tree or heathland thicket, the leaves and flowers support something in the region of one hundred and thirty different species of caterpillar, butterfly, bee, moth and other insects, as well as providing safe nesting for a variety of garden and woodland birds. In the late autumn, the tiny red haws provide them with an essential food source and, if the weather turns harsh in northern Scandinavia, for the arctic thrushes – field fares, red wings and waxwings – which descend in great flocks to strip hedgerows of the last of their autumn colour.

The berries contain antioxidant properties and are widely regarded in Europe as a safe and effective treatment for the early stages of heart disease. The wood has a dense, fine grain and off a tree of decent size, was used for marquetry, boxes and combs. It is excellent fuel, giving off tremendous heat – charcoal from hawthorn was once used for melting pig iron. As a food source, the berries are woefully under-utilised since few people can be bothered to pick them, but for those who do, they are among the best of nature's bounty. A ketchup made from haws adds a certain nimbus to pork; haw jelly is superb with venison and the berries can also be made into jams, syrups, cordials, a delicious, sharp tasting wine and, mixed with crab apples, chutney. Hawthorn berries added to brandy make a winter warmer that seriously rivals sloe gin.

Folklore is kinder to hawthorn, largely, I suspect, because where it was convenient to demonise blackthorn, the early Church could not compete with the role of mayflowers in the pagan festival of Beltane and promptly Christianised hawthorn by claiming it had been used to make the crown of thorns at Christ's crucifixion. Hawthorns were often planted beside wishing wells and in many parts of Ireland, wishing rags or clotties are still tied to them, whilst a custom which endured into the twentieth century was hanging the fresh placenta of a cow or mare on a hawthorn, in the belief that it would protect the mother from post-natal illness.

Henry VII chose a crowned hawthorn bush as his Royal Badge after the identifying circlet worn by Richard III on his helmet was found hanging on one after the battle of Bosworth – hence the expression, 'cleve to thy crown though it hangs on a bush'. Paradoxically there was an absolute conviction among country people that to bring mayflowers into a dwelling place was to tempt misfortune, inevitably leading to sickness and disease. This belief stemmed from the flowers' heady, sickly-sweet scent which has a whiff of necrosis about it, an all-too-familiar smell in an age when corpses were laid out at home for several days prior to burial. Scientists later discovered that the flowers contain trimethylamine, a product of decomposition responsible for the odour when tissue starts to decay.

Our most famous hawthorn is the Glastonbury Thorn, a biflora species which flowers at Christmas and Easter, reputedly grown from the staff of Joseph of Arimathea, uncle of the Virgin Mary. The original tree was burnt by Cromwell's soldiers, but by then there were plenty across Britain grown from cuttings of the original and a sapling from one of these was planted at St John's Church after the Restoration. A sprig of Holy Thorn is customarily sent to the Sovereign each Christmas, a tradition started in the reign of James I.

Dor Hawks

The B6399 from Hawick to Newcastleton meanders through a valley beside a stream known as the Lang Burn. On either side of the road, as it passes intriguing place names like Crib's Hole, Wilson's Shoulder and Brown's Sike, are scrub birch, alder and stunted willow, as well as bracken, rushes and clumps of old, rank heather. Further on, where the road climbs Shankend Shiel, it starts to become enclosed by the western edge of the vast Wauchope Forest, a mix of different ages of larch and spruce with patches of clear fell, forest rides and new plantings. Driving home late on a July evening, on the sort of night moths and Dor beetles bounce off the windscreen and midges become plastered on the Land Rover bonnet, I have often seen a bird resembling a cross between a kestrel and a swallow lift from the rough ground beside the road and flicker away from the headlights into the darkness: a nightjar.

Nightjars, *Caprimulgus europaeus,* or to give them any of their local names – Dor hawks, moth owls, goat suckers, lich fowls or flying toads – are, in my view, our most fascinating and mysterious migrant, more frequently heard than seen. They arrive from Southern Africa in late April and May, dispersing to take up territories in heathland, rough moorland, sand dunes and open woodland, particularly in the southern half of Britain but not uncommonly found in the north and parts of Scotland. On warm summer evenings, as dusk blends into darkness, the male bird sings his extraordinary territorial song, a sustained churring sound, alternating in pitch, which can last up to ten minutes and is not dissimilar to a fishing reel being wound in at different speeds. This song has been analysed to contain around two thousand notes a minute and is only delivered when the bird is perched on a branch or tree stump. As he sings, the bird moves his head from side to side, creating a confusingly ventriloquial effect, which is exacerbated when other nightjars in the vicinity start answering. In flight, the cock occasionally claps his wings together on sighting a hen or to signal alarm and both sexes have a soft *'coowik'* contact call.

The birds are rarely seen in daylight, remaining motionless on the ground amongst bracken and leaf litter, or perched lengthways on a low branch, relying on their incredible camouflage colouring to avoid detection. This takes the form of a pattern of varying whites, greys, buffs and browns, resembling dead leaves or old tree bark. If danger approaches the bird becomes almost reptilian, extending its neck and flattening its body, watching through slitted eyes. When finally flushed, it erupts into the air, clapping its wings in alarm. If protecting a nest or chicks, both cock and hen perform predator-distracting tactics, such as running short distances with a wing down, uttering a guttural hissing; flying off with jerky, discordant wing beats and landing close by; or even lying on the ground and rolling from side to side.

Nightjars are crespucular and at twilight they leave their roosts to forage for food in open rides, moorland fringes, stagnant ponds, marshes and damp meadows near grazing animals. Sometimes they can be seen hawking for insects close to the tree canopy, swooping and hovering in the same company as pipistrelle bats.

Nightjars drink on the wing like swallows and have small, wide, gaping, curved bills surrounded by stiff rictal feathers which assist in catching their diet of virtually any dusk-active insect, from midges to moths and Dor beetles. They also have an unusual serrated middle claw used to remove mites picked up through sitting on the ground during the heat of the day and to straighten the rictal feathers, which can become tangled during preening.

During courtship, the cock glides with wings held in a V above his back, periodically clapping them together and making the contact call while circling the hen. Throughout this display, both rise to a height of about thirty metres, circling rapidly before descending in a fast dive. They then sway and bob to each other, jerking their tails up and down until the hen lowers her head and spreads her wings in supplication.

Once a pair have mated, the hen dispenses with the bother of making a nest and lays her two greyish eggs, blotched with brown markings, among leaf litter and pine needles or simply on the bare earth. Nest sites vary from beneath individual trees or bushes, to the roots of a fallen tree, clear fell areas and mature plantation edges. Birds often return to the same sites annually. Incubation takes about three weeks, with the cock relieving the hen at dawn and dusk to enable her to forage. Both adults feed the chicks during the night with saliva-coated feed balls. Chicks fledge at two and a half weeks and are independent at one month.

Birds in the south nest earlier than those in the north and will generally have time to rear a second brood before the return migration in September. A hen may abandon her nest in prolonged wet weather and, like other ground-nesting birds, the eggs and young are vulnerable to predation from stoats, foxes, badgers, hedgehogs, adders, magpies and crows.

Not surprisingly, these secretive creatures have been the subject of myths and legends for more than a thousand years. Their scientific name – *caprimulgus*, meaning goat sucker – goes back to Roman times and stems from the belief that they suckled goats and poisoned them at the same time. A similar belief was attached to cattle and both were as a result of nightjars taking advantage of the insects that invariably hang around stock. In some parts of Britain, they were thought to be the spirits of children who had died unbaptised and in others, to hear a nightjar presaged death, hence the names lich fowl or corpse bird.

Summering nightjars were once commonly seen throughout Britain but the population declined sharply in the middle of the twentieth century due to a combination of wet summers, habitat loss through afforestation, agricultural reclamations, urban spread and damage to their food source from pesticides. A count by the British Trust for Ornithology in 1981 indicated that the number of churring males was reduced to just over two thousand. Eleven years later, another count showed an increase of fifty per cent. Since then, the number of churring males has risen to four thousand, largely the result of improved forestry management, Countryside Premium and Rural Stewardship Schemes.

If you live near heathland or an area where a block of forestry has been clear-felled, it is well worth braving the midges on a warm, windless night in the hope of hearing one.

A Change in the Season

August can have some of the hottest weather of the year and sometimes the heaviest rainfall. In either event, the days are sultry and the nights heavy and breathless. It is the harvest month and with masterly understatement, folklore pronounces, 'a dry August and warm, does the harvest no harm'. Not to risk over-optimism, this is qualified by, 'if the first week of August be warm, the winter will be long and white'.

Vegetation is at the limit of its growth now and the land begins to look tired as grasses turn brown and leaves darken and wilt, but as the month progresses nature's glorious autumn bounty starts to appear. Blackberries for jam, scarlet haws and rowanberries for jelly, dark purple sloes and damsons for the ever-important sloe gin and, on elder trees, the flower heads die back to be replaced by brilliantly versatile reddish-black elderberries. These can be made into a superb wine similar to port, or used in soufflés, tarts, pies, jellies and muffins. Elderberries can be simmered with sugar to make a syrupy cordial not unlike crème de cassis, and a pint of them stewed with claret, mace, shallots, peppercorns and ginger, bottled and stored in the cellar for a year or more, produces Pontack sauce, an exquisite, spicy condiment for game and cold meat.

Wildlife is showing early signs of preparing for winter. Animals are wandering away from nursery and nest. Birds are moulting and migrating. The cuckoo has already left and, with a last cheery shriek, swifts are suddenly gone. Swallows gather on telephone wires and in the uplands all the summer-nesting waders – redshank, greenshank, snipe, dunlin, lapwing, stonechat, curlew, golden plover and oystercatcher – are flocking and returning to feed on their estuary wintering grounds.

Young mammals such as hedgehog pups, weasel and stoat kits, badger and fox cubs are becoming independent and starting to look for their own hunting territories. Bat pups are fully weaned and able to hunt for midges away from their dams. I am fortunate to have a roost of pipistrelle bats in an old stable block and it is fascinating to watch a stream of adult and juvenile bats dropping like leaves out of a crack in the wall just as the light fades, swooping and diving for midges. Young bats, drawn by the light and the hope of finding food, sometimes come into a house at this time of the year, causing panic and alarm among ladies terrified at the thought of one becoming tangled in their hair. The sensible thing to do on these occasions is to switch off the lights, leave the room and close the door; the bat will soon find its way back out through the window.

August is a frenetic month for insects. There is still plenty of nectar for second-brood butterflies. On chalk downland, Adonis blues and brown argus feed on late-flowering species such as purple field and devil's-bit scabious, pink marjoram, black knapweed, yellow lady's bedstraw and blue harebells. Holly blues may be seen near holly blossom and new brimstones on flowering thistles, the last of the creamy meadowsweet and dog roses, yellow-flowered agrimony and purple betony. Golden gatekeepers and fritillaries bask on woodland edges, feeding on white-flowered cleavers, traveller's joy and yarrow, red dead-nettle, blue cranesbill, pink balsam and herb robert.

Brilliantly iridescent dragonflies, whether long bodied Hawkers or tubby Darters, patrol their territories along river banks where the midges hang thick and meadowsweet, great willowherb, purple loosestrife and yellow flowered irises grow.

Bees, sensing the shortening season, are at their most industrious and it is now that the female worker bees suddenly turn on the drones, abruptly ending their glorious summer of sybaritic idleness, honey-guzzling and occasionally soaring on powerful wings in pursuit of an airborne virgin queen. There is no room in the hive any more for these pampered bachelors and, with biblical ferocity, their sisters drive them out to die in heaps around the hive. With the drones gone, the hive reorganises and the colony prepares for winter.

At some point during the month, usually on a hot day immediately after heavy rain, the air near an ant nest fills with a swarm of flying ants, one of nature's most extraordinary phenomena. These are male ants and new queens which have acquired temporary wings simply to enable them to fly from the host colony, mate and establish a new one elsewhere. Often, several colonies will synchronise swarming and, for a few days, large numbers of airborne mating ants are an even bigger irritation than midges. When mating is over the males die, while the fertilised queen seeks an existing anthill with worker ants that will accept her and look after her eggs and larvae, or she founds a new colony.

The greatest change, of course, is on our heather moorland, where for a few brief weeks the hills are clad in an emperor's cloak and, in the words of Robert Burns, 'The moorcock springs on whirring wings among the blooming heather'. The Twelfth is glorious in every sense of the word. There is no more wonderful sight than thousands of acres of heather in full bloom, and driven grouse are not only the king of game birds, they are unquestionably the most exquisite eating. With the start of the game season, the year has irrevocably turned.

Flankers

Despite some cold springs and often gloomy prognostications about the grouse hatching and chick survival rates, excitement and anticipation for the Glorious Twelfth is as undiminished as ever among guns, moorland managers, keepers, loaders, flankers, beaters, pickers-up and dogs. In August, Britain's heather uplands provide an emperor's cloak of flowering glory, a stunning backdrop to the incomparable sight of the first coveys of the season as they hurtle towards the butts with the wind under their tails.

Small numbers of grouse were first manoeuvred down a regular flight path over a natural obstacle in the landscape, behind which a gun or two were hiding, as early as 1800. The potential for driving rapidly gained momentum, with one of the earliest recorded to a line of guns being on a moor belonging to the Spencer Stanhopes of Cannon Hall, near Barnsley, in 1836. Amongst the guns concealed in sand-holes dug on the moor were Lord Leicester of Holkham and Sir William Cooke of Wheatley, then aged eighty-three and shooting with a flintlock.

Although most moor owners and keepers were working towards the same ends, George Sykes, Captain Henry Savile's keeper at Ryshworth Lodge near Bingley, is credited with developing the science of driving a moor and designing purpose-built 'batteries' or butts. He was responsible for laying out the ground and arranging butt lines on historic moors such as High Force in Teesdale and for advising keepers on many others. Over the next thirty years, grouse moor management was revolutionised and remarkable bags were being achieved on Pennine moors, even before the phenomenal season of 1872, when over seventeen thousand grouse were shot on Wemmergill and just under sixteen thousand on neighbouring High Force.

An experienced beating line operated by a knowledgeable keeper is fascinating to watch. In simplistic terms, the day starts with a drive downwind, lifting birds off their ground towards a natural settling area about threequarters of a mile away over butts built to intercept their usual flight-lines. Each drive, theoretically, feeds birds into the next, and the second drive is taken downwind again, with grouse from the first drive being moved a mile and a half, the maximum range from home they are prepared to fly. The third is a return drive against the wind, taking grouse back to their own ground and is usually the one just before lunch, as grouse, like hill sheep, are never long in returning to the familiar territory of their own hefts.

As a rule, the beating line of a downwind drive starts parallel to the butts and develops into a crescent shape. With a reverse drive, the line should be straight and carried through as fast as possible, without giving birds the opportunity of flying anywhere other than the direction the line is taking. However, few drives are entirely straightforward or driven twice in exactly the same manner; endless imponderables influence the behaviour of grouse as the season progresses, which a keeper must factor into his plans for the day. Wind is, without doubt, the single most important determinant and a minor shift in direction is enough to swing birds away from their normal flight paths. In these conditions, the line pivots accordingly, with one side of the line hanging back or moving forward. I have known occasions when the line of beaters started at right-angles to the butts and used the prevailing wind to swing birds round in a curve over the guns.

Flankers are the unsung heroes of any driven day. Their role is to kneel concealed in the heather, approximately forty yards apart at an angle of forty-five degrees to each end of the line of butts, thus acting as a funnel for the drive and being galvanised into action if birds start veering out. The sudden appearance of flag-waving flankers is often enough to push birds back towards guns and once they have passed, the flankers immediately kneel down and remain hidden until their presence is required again. The essence of successful flanking is surprise, team-work and timing. With a straight downwind drive, it may be enough for the top flanker simply to show himself for birds to move, with the other flankers backing him up only if the birds have not been turned effectively. When the wind is blowing on to the flank or if they are lined out up a steep face, more energetic flagging may be required and success depends on each flanker supporting his neighbour. Birds flying square on to a flank or individual old birds determinedly flying out are impossible to stop and should be left alone. Otherwise there is a risk of spooking coveys flying correctly towards the butts and nothing is more infuriating to guns than birds veering away due to over-enthusiastic flanking.

In the old days, once the drive had started, a keeper had little control other than whistles and flag signals, relying on his flank men to respond individually to each developing situation. Although there is radio communication today between the keeper and the senior flankers, they still have discretion to alter the angle of the flanking line forward or back, depending on how wind and topography influence the birds' behaviour. For example, in a strong crossing wind, the downwind flankers might need to move round at ninety degrees to the butts, while the upwind line falls back to become virtually a continuation of them. Later in the season, birds may choose to settle a hundred yards short of the butts and a couple of flankers, placed strategically forward, can keep them on the move.

To be a successful flanker requires skill and concentration; their work can add considerably to the success or otherwise of a driven day.

Medieval Pets' Names

In the church of St Mary in Clifton Reynes, Buckinghamshire, there is a magnificent altar tomb bearing the crumbling effigies of a medieval knight, Sir Thomas de Reynes and his lady, fashioned from the local Totternhoe stone. Sir Thomas, who died in 1388, lies clad in full armour with his feet resting on a large, bare-skinned, broad-muzzled hound, probably an Alaunt de Boucherie, 'fleet enough to catch a wounded deer, brave enough to hold a wild boar and easily able to dispatch a wolf'. His lady's head rests upon a pillow and at her feet lie a pair of lop-lugged little dogs, perhaps miniature spaniels, the popular 'comforters' of that period.

Dogs symbolised courage, loyalty and vigilance, and appear quite often with effigies of their owners on medieval tombs – there are also two earlier ones of the de Reynes family in St Mary's. A little dog joins Dame Alice Cassey on her early thirteenth century funerary brass in the Saxon church at Deerhurst, in Gloucestershire. There are several others – Cardinal Simon de Langham, for example, who died in 1376, has a pair of dogs on his sepulchre in Westminster Abbey and Robert, Lord Hungerford, executed for his support of the Lancastrian cause in 1464, has a Talbot or perhaps a Gascon hound at his feet on his alabaster ossuary in Salisbury Cathedral. What makes the Alaunt on the tomb of Sir Thomas and the little dog on Dame Alice's funerary brass unusual, and rather special, is that their names, Bo and Tirri, are engraved on their collars. With a little imagination, this immediately brings them to life.

Dogs have been domesticated for at least thirty thousand years and have had a pivotal role in every civilisation. The Iron Age Celts of Britain were great hound breeders and Celtish hounds are mentioned in the works of

Roman historians such as Nemesianus, Arrian, Claudian and Oppian, but it is only in the Middle Ages, when dogs first appear in art and literature, that their names begin to be recorded. Hunting had become a highly stylised, semi-religious, church-blessed occupation and every medieval nobleman's establishment would have a considerable kennel of different breeds, appropriate to hunting the various types of the 'noble beasts of venery'. Amongst the gaze hounds were greyhounds, deerhounds and wolfhounds, as well as large lurchers known as 'bastards' and smaller ones known as 'tumblers'. Scent hounds included the deep-scenting Saint Hubert, Talbots, Gascons, harriers and little kennets. Terriers were used to hunt fox, badger and otter, and a variety of spaniels and setting dogs used in falconry, or to hold birds on the ground whilst a net was drawn over them. Greyhounds and Talbots were the most highly regarded; indeed Edward III had four greyhounds, Tristram, Hector, Brutus and Roland, as his constant companions during his many campaigns. Greyhounds and Talbots were the only hounds used in heraldry, with greyhounds being supporters on the coats of arms of Henry VII, Henry VIII, Mary I and Elizabeth I.

In 1387, Gaston Phoebus, Comte de Foix, one of the greatest huntsmen of the time, who had a kennel of over six hundred hunting dogs, produced the famous classic on medieval hunting, *Le Livre de Chasse*, noted for its exquisite miniature illustrations of hunting. He mentions several hound names such as: Bauderon, Baudelette, Briffault, Cliquau, Fillette, Huielle, Huiaa, Loquebaut and Mirre.

England had effectively been part of France for the previous three hundred years and, although French had been replaced by English following a statute of 1362, there is every reason to suppose that many Anglo-Norman hound names were still in use. Forty years after *Le Livre de Chasse*, Edward of Norwich, Duke of York, produced *The Master of Game*. This was largely an edited translation of Phoebus's work but with five extra chapters specifically on hunting in England and a list of eleven hundred suggested hound names. Among them were Troy,

Blanche, Nosewise, Black Foot, White Foot, Amiable, Nameless, Bowman, Bragg, Brabbler, Laund, Holdfast, Hardy, Sturdy, Greedigut, Ringwood, Absolom, Fletewood, Royster and Ruffler.

If hunting dogs were an essential part of medieval life, so too were the destriers, coursers, jennets, hobbies, palfreys, barbs or rounceys on which their owners rode. Few pet names of medieval horses have come down to us. Most were known by their colour and breed, attached to the name of their owner; for example 'blancart' was a white horse, 'bai' horses with black points were bays, 'baybauson' was a bay horse with white points and 'bayclere' was a bright bay. A grey horse a 'grisel', a dappled grey was a 'pommele', a dark grey was a 'ferraunt', whilst a dappled dark grey was a 'ferraunt pommele'. Mixed coloured horses were roans, as they are today, and a mixed coloured chestnut was a 'ronsorel'. There are a few exceptions: El Cid had a famous horse called Babieca and Baldwin I of Jerusalem was carried to safety after the battle of Ramlah on his mare Gazala. Richard the Lionheart had two favourite horses that he brought back from the crusades – Fauvel, presumably a dun from the name, and Lyard, a white horse; whilst in the metrical romance of Sir Boeve de Haumtone, the knight wins a race on his great horse Arondel against two others who had a half-mile start.

A medieval knight surrounded himself with animals which reflected the attributes he wished to be seen as possessing, these being courage, speed, strength and loyalty. His lady's long, cloistered existence was made bearable by the company of a pet which was a status symbol, a source of amusement and an emotional outlet. Little dogs were the medieval pet *par excellence*, as their frequent appearance in bestiaries indicates.

Toy spaniels and miniature 'singing' beagles were very popular, but the ultimate in designer dog was the Melitaean, a short-muzzled, long-haired dog, the ancestor of the Bichon. They appear often in the iconography of medieval courtly life. Originally the companions of Mediterranean sailors, Melitaeans were natural comics and quickly became fashionable amongst the European nobility. Anne Boleyn had a little dog called Purkoy, a name adapted from the French *pourquoi*, because of its naturally inquisitive expression. The dog had originally belonged to Lady Honor Lisle, wife of the governor of Calais, and was in all probability a Melitaean. Match coursing was a popular spectator sport among noble ladies and Anne also had a favourite greyhound, Urian, given to her by the courtier William Brereton and named after his brother, Sir Urian. Poor Anne – Purkoy was killed under suspicious circumstances a few weeks before she was beheaded. Meanwhile William Brereton was among those, including her brother, George, accused of having intercourse with her and subsequently sentenced to be hanged, drawn and quartered.

The Duchess of Suffolk, a lady-in-waiting to Queen Catherine Parr, named her toy spaniel Gardiner, after the unpopular Roman Catholic bishop, Stephen Gardiner, whom she loathed. Catherine was an outspoken supporter of the English Reformation and caused much amusement to other followers whenever she scolded 'Gardiner' to heel or called him ridiculous names.

A succession of pet dogs provided solace to Mary Queen of Scots during her long years as a prisoner of the Earl of Shrewsbury in Tutbury Castle, Wingfield Manor, Chatsworth and Sheffield Castle. During this period, Mary passed much of the time engaged in embroidery and there is a collection of work made by her (and Bess of Hardwick) in the Victoria and Albert Museum, known as the Oxburgh Hangings. This collection includes an image of a little brown and white dog called Jupiter, but Mary's most famous dog, of course, is Geddon. Reputed to be a Skye terrier, but almost certainly a Melitaean, Geddon emerged from Mary's petticoats after she had been executed to lie, whimpering, between her shoulders. Poor Geddon never recovered from the loss of his mistress and soon pined away.

Generic names for other animals have come down to us: 'Gyb' for a tomcat and 'Tybalt' or 'Tibert' for a she-cat, hence tabby. The bird we know as a magpie was originally a 'pie' from its pied colour and acquired the 'mag' from the name given to a chattering woman. Sparrows, immortalised in John Skelton's fifteenth century poem, *The Boke of Phyllyp Sparrowe*, were 'Pip' or 'Phillip' and red squirrels, a popular ladies' pet, feature extensively in medieval art either on leads or being carried, kept their French name, 'Fouquet', as did green parakeets, known as 'Pierres'. Monkeys were invariably called 'Roberts'. Both parrots (or 'popinjays') and monkeys were popular pets among the very rich; parrots were seen as a symbol of purity and are often portrayed in religious bestiaries. A pair are carved on a misericord in Wells Cathedral and two parrots were the companions of Elizabeth de Burgh, wife of King Robert Bruce, during her twenty years of imprisonment by the English.

When it comes to pets, nothing much has changed since 1570, when Dr John Caius wrote: '...we English men are marvailous greedy gaping gluttons after novelties, and covetous cormorants of things that be seldom rare, strange and hard to get...'.

Goose Fever

During August, it is not unknown for me to show distinct signs of goose fever, a malady which begins to afflict wildfowlers at this time of year, reaching its peak by 1st September, the opening day of the season, and then recurring fairly frequently until 20th February, when the season closes. The early symptoms always follow the same pattern: old and well-loved books by authors and hunter naturalists such as Abel Chapman, Arthur Cadman, Sir Ralph Payne-Galway or Colonel Peter Hawker pile up on my bedside table and, in particular, those by Denys Watkins-Pitchford, better known as BB.

I have read BB's beautifully evocative *Tide's Ending*, *Dark Estuary*, *Recollections of a Longshore Gunner*, his wildfowling essays in the Bedside series and the recently published *The Confessions of a Coastal Gunner* countless times, but they have never lost their fascination or ability to set the heart racing.

As the fever builds, other symptoms will include studying the lunar cycles, which influence the movements of wildfowl, from September until the end of February. Contacting wildfowling friends, whom one may not have spoken to since the end of last season, and making plans to meet them at estuaries such as Dornoch, Montrose Bay, the Tay, the Nith, Lindisfarne, Morecambe Bay, Gedney Drove End, Wells-next-the-Sea or any of the other saltmarsh destinations up and down the country to which wildfowlers make their seasonal pilgrimage.

Goose fever is easily diagnosed; it is a longing for the stark winter beauty of mudflats and foreshore, saltmarshes and river estuaries, the iodine scent of the sea and the distant rumble of surf, but, above all, the music of wildfowl.

Living in the Borders, I am well placed for the Solway, Lindisfarne, Morecambe Bay, Aberlady or even the Tay and there was a time when I would be out on the foreshore somewhere without fail to greet the dawn of the new season. Now I wait and watch nature for signs that weather is hardening in the sub-arctic, bringing the autumn and the grey geese south from their summer nesting grounds in Greenland and Iceland.

The change from the vibrancy of summer to autumn's sombre colours always seems so dramatic. In the middle of the month, sunrise is half an hour later, there is a noticeable drop in temperature, insect life plummets and there is always one particular morning when the familiar screeching of swallows hunting for midges round the farm buildings suddenly ceases. Simultaneously, all the summer moorland nesting migrants – such as curlews, plover, snipe, oystercatchers and redshanks – disappear. They have been slipping away individually or in small flocks for a couple of weeks, but their sudden and complete absence always comes as a shock. Plants die back to their roots or turn to seed; mushrooms and toadstools appear; the leaves of deciduous trees become tinged with yellow; and the winged seeds of ash, sycamore and field maple start helicopering down, while acorns, beech mast and conkers in their spiky green shells litter the ground under oak, beech and horse chestnut trees.

Every night in the week running up to the autumn equinox, which traditionally begins on 21st September, St Matthew's Day, my old dog and I stand in the moonlight listening for geese flying along the Tweed corridor from Berwick-on-Tweed to the Solway. Pink-footed geese migrate ahead of the larger greylag in early September and as each successive wave arrives in northern Scotland, the previous one moves south, with as many as sixty-five thousand building up in the Montrose Basin and perhaps thirty thousand in the Solway during the month. Over the next few weeks, vast numbers will settle on estuaries down the east and west coasts, with a particular concentration in north

Norfolk, where they feed on the sugar beet tops left behind by the beet harvesters. I always receive progress reports from 'fowlers in the north as the great armadas of birds move down through Scotland, but when I hear the thrilling sound of the 'Gabriel Hounds' calling to each other as they fly over the farm, I know that with the equinoctial storms approaching, the time has come to put my 'fowling gear together.

The modern wildfowler tends to favour a 12-bore semi-automatic, chambered for 3½-inch magnum cartridges, weighing about 7½ pounds for geese, such as the new Remington 887 NitroMag. I, on the other hand, use my old single-barrelled 8-bore hammer gun weighing 13 pounds, with its Jones patent rotary under-lever, rebounding back-action lock and 34-inch Damascus barrel, made by E.M. Reilly of Oxford Street and Rue Scribe, Paris, in 1885.

Reilly was among gunsmiths such as Tolley, Ford, Greener, Wilkes or Lewis, who specialised in making big bore 'fowling guns and mine would once have belonged to a market gunner, using his knowledge of the influence of wind, tide and moon on the movements of wildfowl to make a lonely living out on the marshes. It is a lump to lug about and non-toxic bismuth cartridges cost a fiver each, but I cherish it because shooting with the same guns as the old longshoremen is, for me, as much a part of the mystique of wildfowling as the lonely estuaries, the morning melody of a thousand waking waterfowl and the unpredictable habits of the geese.

Waiting for the dawn on the edge of a saltmarsh, I am often reminded of the aphorism, copied from a grave in Cumberland and used by BB to preface his books:

> *The wonder of the world; The beauty and the power*
> *The shapes of things; Their colours, lights and shades*
> *These I saw; Look ye also whilst life lasts.*

Autumn

The Wheel Turns

The wheel of the seasons turns from summer to autumn in September. Daylight hours are inexorably shortening and in the cool early mornings mist hangs in the valley bottoms, grass is sodden with dew and every spider's web glistens with tiny droplets of moisture. There is a massive drop in insect activity during the first weeks of the month, except among bees searching for the last available nectar, and wasps. Wasps spend all summer assiduously hunting smaller insects for their queen's larvae, which, in return, provide a sugar-rich saliva on which the adults feed. Now that the breeding cycle is over, they search for any food containing sugar and, until cold weather kills them off, become an unpopular kitchen pest.

Insects die off and the familiar screeching and twittering of the previous four months suddenly ceases as swallows and house-martins depart on the long journey back to Africa. This cheery summer song is replaced by the yapping of geese flying in high skeins as they migrate to their winter feeding grounds. There is no more thrilling sound than that of the 'Gabriel Hounds' flying by moonlight above our farm in the Borders, on the last leg of their route from Svalbard to the Solway.

September is a magical month for sportsmen; wildfowl and partridge come into season on the 1st and salmon move into their upper beats, providing exciting back-end fishing. As the month progresses, most plants die back to their roots or turn to seed – thistles and rosebay willowherb, for example – leaving a few hardy specimens such as yellow toadflax, fleabane and bird's-foot trefoil to add a little colour to hedgerows and damp places, while purple loosestrife, wild angelica and the invasive Himalayan balsam still flourish along river banks. The leaves of deciduous trees now become tinged with yellow, the winged seeds of sycamore, field maple and ash helicopter through the air, whilst acorns, beech mast and conkers in their spiky green shells litter the ground under oak, beech or horse chestnut trees.

Autumn's bounty fills the hedgerows: with blackberries, rose hips, sloes, elderberries, crab apples and hazelnuts, which once were an important source of winter protein. From medieval times until the early nineteenth century, Holy Cross Day, 14th September, was traditionally Nutting Day, a festival when whole communities would disappear into the woods to harvest the nuts. Nutting Day was an opportunity for teenagers to escape the watchful eye of their parents and among the many myths and legends associated with this event, was the superstition that 'the Devil goes a-nutting on Holyrood Day'. Apparently he was often disguised as an irresistibly charming gentleman, and was entirely to blame for 'the Devil's babies', born the following June.

Nothing is more synonymous with autumn than the mushrooms, toadstools and other fungi that appear in woodland or old pasture during September, sprouting up among leaf litter, decaying stumps, the trunks of trees or simply emerging as jelly, oozing out of the ground. These prehistoric, parasitic growths, lacking the ability to produce their own food, absorb sustenance from living or dead plant matter, creating a nutrient recycling process without which crops, trees and grass would not survive. There are around twenty thousand fungi in Britain and what we see at this time of the year are the fruiting bodies, a device for distributing spores; the fungus itself is a mass of filamentous growths, extending beneath the soil or whatever happens to be the host matter.

A number of these fantastical growths – described so succinctly by Shelley as 'pale, fleshy, as if the decaying dead with a spirit of growth had been animated' – are extremely good to eat. Apart from field mushrooms, there are little stumpy *Boletus edulis*, or ceps, which grow in coniferous forests; chanterelles, which appear in sheets of egg-yolk yellow among mosses in deciduous woodland; and horns of plenty clustering in leaf litter. Shaggy ink caps are arrayed on compost and dung-heaps. Then there are puffballs and parasols; wood and field blewits; wrinkled, pale-skinned morels; delicate, silver-grey oyster mushrooms; and chicken of the woods, bulging in gibbous-tiered groups from the trunks of oak, cherry or sweet chestnut trees. Regrettably, many others contain deadly toxins and, unless one is entirely certain of identification, it is as well to remember John Gerard, apothecary to James I, who warned, 'Most of them do strangle and suffocate the eater'!

The temperature drops and the weather changes on St Matthew's Day, 21st September, with the start of the autumn equinox: 'St Matthew brings cold rain and dew. St Matthew shuts up the bees.' This is the period of gales, heavy rain and flooding, as Atlantic depressions deepen and land temperatures cool faster than those at sea, creating a build-up of water vapour. The approach of the equinox is an anxious period for apple growers harvesting their orchards before the weather spoils the crop: 'September blow soft, 'til the fruit is in the loft.' By now, the last of the wheat harvest is in and on Michaelmas Day, the 29th, landlords traditionally held the annual rent audit and entertained their tenants. Geese fattened on harvest gleanings would be served: 'September, when by custom (right divine), geese are ordained to bleed at Michael's shrine.'

Morecambe Bay Shrimps

M orecambe Bay is broad, shallow, beautiful and deadly. It is a place of quicksands and fearsome tidal bores that travel faster than a galloping horse; a place where the sea recedes an incredible eight miles to expose an immense one-hundred-square-mile 'wet Sahara' of sand and mudflats, divided by ever changing patterns of water-filled channels and gullies, meandering into the hazy distance. For centuries, fishermen from the little villages round the Lancashire and Cumbrian coasts have fished this bay for flounders, bass, cod or whitebait. At low tide a treasure trove of cockles and mussels is uncovered and, in the deeper channels, brown shrimps – Morecambe Bay's unique contribution to British cuisine, the iconic potted shrimp.

Potting meat, fish or poultry in fat, oil or butter used to be a common method of preserving food before refrigeration and until about 1850, potted shrimps were a delicacy exclusive to the area around Morecambe Bay. Local fishermen trudged across the sands at low tide carrying six-foot-wide hand nets mounted on a pole and caught shrimps trapped in the shallow gullies and gutters. These were potted in butter and sold from handcarts door-to-door round the Bay villages.

When the railway from Lancaster reached Grange-over-Sands on the Cumbrian coast in 1857, Morecambe Bay suddenly became the holiday destination for wealthy Victorians and the demand for potted shrimps rocketed, not just in the smart hotels and villas being built all round the coast, but in London too. To keep up the supply, fishermen had to find a way of accessing the deeper channels and, for many years, the solution was larger nets pulled behind a horse and cart. At one time, as many as eighty-six horse-drawn shrimping rigs were in use, but by the 1950s the right sort of aquatic cart horse had become hard to find and they were gradually replaced by tractors. Sadly, there are now only a handful of hardy souls prepared to operate the tractors, one of whom is Les Salisbury, the champion of the potted shrimp and the man responsible for keeping their tradition alive.

The seventh generation of fishermen to follow the family tradition, Les was helping his grandfather and uncles as a little boy in the days when brown shrimps were still caught in horse-drawn nets. Peeling and potting shrimps in clarified butter was a cottage industry, involving every member of the fishing families; when Les came home from school, there was often a pile of shrimps on the kitchen table waiting to be peeled before he could go out to play. In 1983, he started his award-winning company, Furness Fish, Poultry and Game Supplies, potting shrimps under the brand name 'Morecambe Bay Potted Shrimps'. Having spent twenty-eight years building up his business and becoming a familiar figure at London's Borough Market and at shows such as Burley, Badminton, Lowther or the CLA Game Fair, Les has retired from the business to return to his first love, fishing. His niece, Clare Worrall, who had worked for Les for the previous fifteen years, purchased the business and is now carrying on the family tradition.

On the shingle above the high water line at Bardsea, a tiny village three miles from Ulverston, Les's pride and joy, a much customised, rust-dappled fifty-year-old Nuffield, is parked beside a couple of equally elderly tractors and a collection of narrow, four-wheeled trailers piled with nets, ropes and fish boxes. 'They don't make them like this any more,' said Les, giving this monument to post-war engineering an affectionate pat. 'Modern ones can't take the punishment. Anything made after about 1970 would just fall to bits.' With a series of tortured groans, the Nuffield was coaxed into life and started belching smoke. We hitched on a trailer and with a crunching of gears, chugged down the beach and onto the sands.

Speed seemed to be of the essence and we bucketed along flat out in top gear with the throttle lever pulled back, weaving our way between soft and hard sand or bouncing through water-filled gullies in a cloud of spray. The shore line soon disappeared and we were in a weird world of vague horizons, screaming gulls, rippled sand and shallow pools of water.

Three miles into this vast damp wilderness, where tractors, trailers, horses and indeed, humans, have been known to disappear without trace, we arrived at the Ulverston Channel, a deep, fast-flowing tidal river that divides the sands. Here, the trailer was uncoupled and the two fifteen-foot-wide trawl nets hooked on behind. These have narrow mouths, kept open by a rectangular metal frame and mesh that tapers down to a fine gauge in the tail. The trailer was re-attached to a long rope, all two hundred and twenty feet of it, and the front wheels set at a slant; when the rope tightened as we drove off parallel to the channel, the trailer was then pulled at right-angles into deep water. The funnel nets fill out behind it and, as they are dragged along, the bottom bar of the rectangular net mouth scrapes the bed of the channel, disturbing the brown shrimps lurking in the uppermost layer of sand. They jump up to avoid the advancing bar and are swept into the tail of the net.

'This is the boring bit', Les muttered, as we churned slowly along in the warm, early September sunshine, water pouring over the footplates and the trailer submerged from view. Surreal perhaps – the tide was moving at the same speed as the tractor, giving the impression we were static – but never boring. Les is a fascinating mine of information about the history of shrimping and the difficulties involved in providing a much sought-after luxury product.

There are two shrimping seasons; the spring run from April until June, when it becomes too hot, and the autumn run, from September until the first frosts in November. 'It's a different world out here in November, imagine what it's like when the wind and rain come howling in off the Irish Sea.'

There are only eight or nine shrimp fishermen left now and where once shrimping was generational, very few young people are following in their fathers' footsteps. One of the reasons for this is the popularity of cockles and mussels. Cockles can be dug out of the sand and mussels harvested with relative ease and at little cost, compared to maintaining the vintage tractors, repairing nets, physically catching the shrimps in all weathers, cooking and peeling them, all for the princely sum of £13.00 per pound. A major problem is finding anyone still prepared to peel the shrimps; an experienced peeler will peel a pound and a half an hour, which roughly equates to 450 shrimps, for which the going rate is £3.50 per pound weight.

Shrimpers normally travel in pairs for safety in case of a breakdown or getting bogged; so it was some relief when another tractor and trailer appeared, driven by Ray Porter, one of the two official Queen's Guides to the Sands. The office of Queen's Guide is a Royal Appointment dating back to 1536, when the Bay was a major transport route and those with intimate knowledge of the treacherous sands were officially appointed to guide parties across at low tide. Nowadays, Ray takes groups of enthusiasts over the sands from Ulverston to Chapel Island at Flookburgh.

After a long drag, the tractors were driven out on to the sand and the nets emptied into fish boxes. A writhing, heaving mass of crabs, tiny jellyfish, whitebait, flukes, the occasional Weever fish (with their vicious, poisonous dorsal fins which can put a fisherman off work for days), and hundreds of translucent brown shrimps. These were shaken through riddles until only the correct size of shrimp remained. Ray does this by hand, using an old-fashioned garden sieve, whilst Les has a splendid homemade contraption driven by an electric motor, mounted on one of the tractor mudguards. Everything is done in a rush now. It is vital the shrimps are cooked before they die, otherwise they become soggy and difficult to peel. As soon as the riddling was finished, nets and ropes were packed away and we careered back to the beach at maximum speed. The boxes of shrimps were quickly transferred to Les's truck and we hurried round the coast to Furness's business premises at Flookburgh.

Here the shrimps were tipped into a vat of boiling seawater and as they rose to the surface, a carpet of pinky-brown crustacea, they were scooped onto aluminium trays, chilled and taken to the peeling room. To cope with the lack of hand peelers, Les invested in four peeling machines costing £50,000 each, invented by an eccentric Dutch shrimper who spent a lifetime trying to solve the problem of peeling by hand. These machines can grade and peel up to twenty pounds of shrimps an hour, but any too big for the machines are still peeled by one of the staff. Holding a little shrimp between forefinger and thumb, breaking off the tail and drawing the body from the carapace looks surprisingly easy, but it takes at least eight months of practice to become even reasonably proficient.

Brown shrimps, *Crangon crangon*, unlike the ubiquitous pink shrimp, *Pandalus borealis*, are unique in their capacity to absorb butter and the next process is to cook them. Fifteen-pound batches of shrimps are simmered for fifteen minutes in twelve pounds of melted butter, mixed with a secret combination of spices, including mace, nutmeg and cayenne pepper, drained, chilled, potted and the pots sealed with fresh melted butter.

Clare Worrall buys most of the catch from the few remaining Morecambe Bay shrimp fishermen and other sources, processing two thousand tubs, each containing about forty shrimps, every day. Apart from Furness's presence at Borough Market, country shows, horse trials and food fairs, potted and loose peeled shrimps are sold by mail order or directly to Booths, the north of England's superb supermarket chain, Harrods, Fortnum & Mason, Waitrose, Sainsbury's, Selfridges and other quality food outlets.

Potted shrimps are a national treasure, as closely associated with Britain as roast beef, the Union Jack, cricket, bell-ringing or foxhunting. A versatile delicacy, they are as acceptable at breakfast as for an entrée to a grand lunch or dinner. They are the essential ingredient of a picnic or a shooting tea and capable of transforming scrambled eggs into a gastronomic nimbus. Enjoy them while you may; Les and his Nuffield won't be around forever.

St Anthony's Fire

Among our poisonous fungi that appear in the autumn on acid swampy soil or among deciduous woodland – gibbous death or panther caps, orange fly agaric, shrivelled red-staining Inocybes, shiny brown roll-rim or the ochre-coloured *cortinarius speciosissimus* that resemble chanterelles but ruin your kidneys – none are as deadly or innocuous-looking as the ergot.

Claviceps purpurea start life in early summer as tiny, pale pink drumstick shaped fruit, whose threadlike spores are carried by the wind to flowers of a wide variety of weed grasses, particularly black grass and rye species. By autumn, as these plants ripen, some of the kernels appear as small, elongated black seeds, similar in shape to mouse droppings. These are the sclerotia and they contain a number of alkaloids that are massively toxic. Ever since cereal production began in Mesopotamia, nine thousand years before Christ, providing further host plants for ergot, these little sclerotia have found their way into the food chain and have been the cause of hundreds of thousands of agonising deaths. Unfortunately, it was not until the nineteenth century that anyone made the association between the deadly blackened seeds found amongst rye, the principal cereal of the poor, but also to some extent in wheat and barley, and the appalling consequences of their unwitting consumption.

Ergotomine poisoning affects both humans and livestock by paralysing the motor nerve endings and restricting the flow of blood to the extremities. Grazing animals are less at risk, as ergot matures at the point grass ceases to be palatable and is usually dislodged by the movement of stock as they feed. Those that do ingest even the smallest quantity collapse with staggers and their tails, ears, lips and hooves can slough off.

Humans who become infected through bread made from contaminated flour experience violent convulsions, wrenching muscle contractions leading to abortion, an agonising sensation of burning, terrifying hallucinations, gangrene and loss of limbs. Lucretius referred to this horrible malady as *ignis infernalis*, hell's fire, the term used by early Christian monks who first recorded the epidemics that swept across Europe. In 857, a great plague of swollen blisters and loathsome rot consumed the people of the Rhine valley, so that their limbs dropped off before death. In Paris, wailing and writhing men collapsed in the street during the autumn of 945, others fell over vomiting and shouting 'Fire, I'm burning!'. Fifty years later, a ghastly pestilence devastated Rome and the surrounding district, a hidden fire that separated flesh from the bones and consumed it. In the first hundred years of the millennium, fifty thousand men, women and children across France went berserk, dying in unbearable pain.

Towards the end of this period a nobleman, Gaston de la Valloire, founded a hospice for sufferers near the Church of St Anthony at Saint Didier de la Mothe where the saint's remains were buried; this was out of gratitude for his son's remarkable recovery. The church became a shrine for pilgrims, either brain-damaged or affected with gangrene, and its altar became piled with two-dimensional silver effigies of afflicted limbs, sold to sufferers by reliquary hawkers lurking outside.

So prevalent were outbreaks of the sickness, now known as St Anthony's Fire, that a total of three hundred and seventy hospices, painted bright red for easy identification, were built across Europe and Britain over the next five hundred years. One was erected in 1430 as far north as Leith in Scotland. Hospital Brothers of St Anthony, tending the sick who dragged themselves to these refuges, could offer little by way of comfort other than to anoint their blackened stumps with lard, dose them with concoctions made from chicory or lovage and bolster their spirits by assuring them that both Christ and St Anthony's sufferings had been just as bad.

Ergot thrives after cold winters followed by wet springs. The Little Ice Age of the Middle Ages provided ideal conditions, with sporadic outbreaks every ten years or so, when whole rural communities were wiped out through eating infected bread. What are now believed to be mass infections of ergotism were often confused with the plague. The dancing manias synonymous with the Black Death and their associated mortalities were almost certainly hallucinogenic symptoms of ergot. Others affected by it became victims during the persecution of witches in the sixteenth and seventeenth centuries. Probably the best documented of these were the Salem Witch Trials of 1692, when one hundred and fifty people from Essex and Fairfax counties in Connecticut were accused of witchcraft. Of these, nineteen were hung and one accidentally crushed to death under interrogation before the Governor of Massachusetts, Sir William Phips, put a stop to the trials.

Despite wheat replacing rye as the staple flour for bread, incidents of death through ergotamine poisoning continued wherever cereals were grown. There was an outbreak of dancing mania in southern New England in 1714. According to Sun Insurance company records, eight people died of St Anthony's Fire in London during December 1720. Of more historical import was the decimation of Peter the Great's army, poised at Astrakhan for the invasion of Turkey. The first Cossack ponies started to collapse in August 1722 and by the end of the autumn, when the invasion was called off, twenty thousand men had died. Another outbreak of gangrenous ergotism at Sologne, in north-central France, killed eight thousand people in the winter of 1777. The infectious hysteria following this disaster is considered by many to be the spark that ignited the French Revolution.

One of the more bizarre incidents of assumed ergotism occurred on the 280-ton half brig Mary Celeste, which left New York for Genoa on 7th November 1872 with a crew of eight, plus the Master's wife and daughter, and was found empty and undamaged one month later. In the last eighty years there have been three major incidents, one in southern

Russia during 1927 when ten thousand victims lost their lives. That same year, one hundred and eighty-five people amongst the Jewish community of Manchester were severely affected; whilst in 1951, two hundred people in the town of Pont-St-Esprit suffered severe symptoms, of whom thirty-two went insane and four died.

Curiously, although no one connected sclerotia in crops as the cause of these disasters, herbalists and midwives did recognise that they contained certain medical properties, particularly in assisting difficult pregnancies by inducing uterine contractions. Regardless of the extreme difficulty in administering non-toxic doses, the use of sclerotia gained entry into academic history for this purpose in 1808, only to be smartly removed fourteen years later when Dr Hosack, the famous New York physician, condemned it as the cause of escalating childbirth-related deaths.

Traces of ergot were among the two hundred types of herbal seed and plant remains found amongst ancient hospital waste and surgical off-cuts during an archeological investigation at the Hospice of Soutra in the Scottish Borders, built in 1164 and once the largest centre of healing in northern Britain.

Researchers in the 1940s isolated the psychoactive ingredient in ergot which creates hallucinations and produced the drug LSD. This was seized upon by the CIA as the definitive truth drug for interrogation, until experiments on unsuspecting US servicemen proved it to be not only completely useless for this purpose, but also extremely dangerous. LSD became the cult drug of the 1960s and those of us who were around at the time will remember the tragedies that were the consequence of a bad 'trip'. Not least of these was the Irish aristocrat immortalised in The Beatles' Sergeant Pepper album, who 'didn't notice that the lights had changed'. Today, ergotamine derivatives are used in medication to control migraines and post-partum haemorrhaging.

Nowadays there are stringent safety practices for screening grain, to guarantee that no ergot enters the food chain. Producers try to ensure that seed grain is completely free of weed grasses. However, ergot remains a cereal grower's nightmare and the complicated process to extract it from a contaminated crop of course dramatically downgrades the value. Modern conservation practices which benefit bio-diversity – such as not spraying field margins for grass weeds and the facility that allows broad headlands to be accepted as set-aside – have accelerated an increase in ergot. After years of research, BASF, the giant chemical company, has at last produced a seed treatment called Kinto, which under laboratory testing has proved successful in inhibiting the growth of the ergot fungus. Watch out though: there's a lot of it about.

Weather Lore

September is such a strange month. In the first couple of weeks the countryside still has the heavy verdancy of summer; swallows swoop screeching back and forth, hunting midges round our farm buildings; yellow wagtails follow sheep in the hill parks, feeding on insects disturbed by their grazing. The heather is in the last throes of glorious, wine-red colour and the moorland migrants that nest in the hills every summer – snipe, curlews, plovers, oystercatchers, wheatears and stonechats – are all still in exuberant evidence.

I have often sat out on the marshes at the start of the wildfowling season, waiting for the afternoon tide flight, surrounded by gnats, with a combine harvester rumbling up and down in the field behind me. In the middle of the month, though, everything suddenly changes; sunrise is half an hour later and there is a noticeable drop in temperature. In the mornings, the valley bottoms are often shrouded in wraiths of mist and the moorland is covered in a carpet of shimmering white silk, stretching unbroken as far as the eye can see. Here and there, a patch of woodland or a stone sheep stell shows up like a shadowy island and the only signs of livestock are the faint, dark lines where sheep have moved downhill towards their low-ground grazing.

This incredible phenomenon is created by the dew-laden sheet webs of millions of tiny *Linyphiidae* spiders, festooning every heather plant, tussock and clump of rushes. Centuries ago, medieval shepherds believed these fragile webs caused a fatal affliction of sheep known as 'braxy' and drove their flocks into enclosures at night for protection. As the sun comes up and the dew dries, the moor regains its natural colours and the air becomes full of gossamer strands gliding in the breeze, each carrying a juvenile spider, leaving home and travelling to a new feeding and breeding territory. They become airborne by climbing to the tip of a plant, raising their abdomens, exuding a filament of web and floating off on a current of warm air. Sometimes they land within a few yards but can also be swept up to enormous heights, parachuting down miles away from the launch area. If the wind is in the wrong direction, vast numbers find themselves carried out to sea.

The transition between summer and autumn always seems so clearly defined; the first equinoctial storms strip the flowers off heather, the edges of leaves on the oaks and ash trees behind the house start to turn yellow and bracken fronds begin to dry and curl up. Salmon move through to the upper beats and the coats of young fox cubs lose their greyish tint, becoming redder and more adult. Suddenly, the summer migrants all seem to disappear; individually or in flocks they have gradually been slipping away for some weeks, but their final absence and the void of silence they leave behind comes as an abrupt shock. The hedgerows fill with colour as berries ripen: blackberries, wild raspberries, rosehips, haws, elderberries and sloes. Meanwhile our kitchen reeks of jam and hot vinegar.

Out on the moor, the rowan tree by the ruins of an old shieling cottage turns a glorious scarlet. Robins and wrens start their winter territorial songs; flocks of fieldfares squabble noisily as they hunt for grassland insects; charms of goldfinches delicately feed on thistle-heads. Sometimes, on a clear night, if I am listening for skeins of geese moving along the Tweed corridor to the Solway, I hear the penetrating flight calls of redwings on their migration from Scandinavia.

There is a sense of urgency among wildlife at this time of year, as the food source for many of them diminishes. After a summer of sybaritic ease, drone bees are brutally evicted from their hives and creatures that go into partial hibernation – bats, toads, snakes, hedgehogs and the smaller mammals – are feeding hard to put on body fat for winter. The intake now, for those that have had second litters or were late born, will be the difference between life and death. Jays, grey squirrels and our few remaining reds start to hoard acorns and beechnuts; mushrooms and toadstools start to emerge and, on warm evenings, the last scents of summer flowers are mixed with a faint whiff of decay.

I watch the change in nature more closely during September than any other month. Like most countrymen, especially wildfowlers, I yearn for a hard winter and seek to interpret every nuance in animal behaviour and the abundance or dearth of autumn wild-plant growth as indications of weather to come: the fat round a rabbit's kidneys, the date the pink feet and widgeon arrive at Lindisfarne or when the grouse start to pack.

What is so extraordinary about these earnest annual prognoses is that I know they will have absolutely no bearing on how the winter develops. The profusion of nuts and berries is entirely due to heat or rain at the crucial period in a plant's development; a healthy rabbit should be fat in the autumn; grouse normally start to pack in late September; and there is little difference in the movement of summer and winter migrants from year to year. I sometimes wonder why the mystique of weather folklore still has such significance for country people. It is partly a reluctance to lose the romance associated with changing seasons, but perhaps we also share the primitive anxiety that affects wildlife; a need to prepare for the worst.

Athena

The High Weald of Kent and Sussex, with its endless succession of little hills and steep-sided ghylls covered in chestnut and oak trees is still, despite pressure from urbanisation, one of the most beautiful parts of England. The patchwork of small fields surrounded by overgrown hedges between woods and shaws are stiff with reminders of the old iron ore industry, cannon foundries and Wealden iron masters, like Ralph Hugget and Mad Jack Fuller. At dusk one evening, I was walking near a silted-up pond that once provided power to drive a foundry hammer, when I saw what appeared to be a woodcock lolloping along the hedge line. It was only when it settled on a gate post and then emitted a sound similar to a children's party hooter, blown with vigour, that I recognised a little owl.

These comic little birds are the smallest owl in Britain, scarcely larger than a thrush. The plumage is golden-buff, mottled and barred with white, silver and black. They have rounded wings, long, slender, feathery legs and a short tail. The facial disc is flat, white and surrounded by a heart shaped black border. Their eyes are bright yellow with black pupils, surmounted by bushy white brows, giving a perpetually outraged expression. This impression of diminutive rage is enhanced by their habit of bobbing up and down and shaking their tail if approached on one of their day-time perches, be it gate post, telegraph pole, low branch or crevice in a ruined building. They are active by night but do most of their hunting at dawn and dusk, for a diet that is largely insectivorous, consisting of crane flies, cock-chafers and other beetles, moths, earthworms, slugs, snails, earwigs and some small mammals – voles, shrews, field mice and, occasionally, lizards and frogs. During the breeding season, this list may also include small birds, ranging from sparrows to blackbirds.

The flight of a little owl is low and undulating, as it searches for food or swoops from perch to perch. They prefer open lowland farms, orchards, moorland fringes and parks with scattered old trees. They are noisy birds with a variety of different calls, ranging from the petulant yelps of a lapdog to prolonged reedy mewing; and they become very vocal indeed during the breeding season (February to March) as the males establish territories. Once paired up, male and female frequently call alternately in a duet which I find enchanting, but others find incessant and harsh. In France, 'to cry like a little owl' is a term of reproach.

Little owls rely on natural nesting sites – a hollow tree, derelict farm buildings, quarries and sometimes rabbit burrows – in which to lay their eggs. Incubation takes about four weeks from late April and is undertaken by the female, whilst the male hunts for himself, his mate and the young. Once the brood of three to five owlets can tear food for themselves, the female is free to hunt at a time when growth rate is critical. The young fledge at around five weeks but continue to be fed by the parent birds for another few weeks until they are independent and able to hunt for themselves.

Although little owls are probably the most frequently seen owl in England and Wales, they are a comparatively recent introduced species. *Athena Noctua* and its related sub-species have a distribution that extends from France across the Middle East to Asia and south into North Africa. They are particularly associated with the Greek goddess Pallas Athene and traditionally nested in the masonry of the Acropolis. Little owls are listed by the early nineteenth century ornithologists Bewick (1809), Mudie (1835) and MacGillivray (1840) as rare vagrant visitors but imported birds were commonly available from dealers as pets – they were easily tamed and popular for controlling cockroaches.

The first attempt to naturalise them was made by the delightfully eccentric naturalist, Charles Waterton of Walton Hall in Yorkshire: he purchased twelve birds in Rome in July 1842, believing that their introduction would be 'particularly useful to the British horticulturist'.

After an arduous ten-month journey, during which seven birds died (five of cold, following an attempt by Waterton to give them a warm bath) the survivors were liberated into the park at Walton, never to be seen again.

There are isolated records of vagrant birds over the next thirty years, before the next venture at naturalisation, when Colonel Meade-Waldo started releasing little owls at Stonewall Park, near Edenbridge in Kent, 'to rid belfries of sparrows and bats, and fields of mice' (as described by Christopher Lever in *The Naturalised Animals of Britain and Ireland*). Between 1874 and 1880 about forty birds were turned down and one nest confirmed in 1879. More birds were released over the four years from 1896 and, by the turn of the century, the Colonel was writing that he knew of forty nests between Sevenoaks and Tunbridge Wells. Meanwhile, in Northamptonshire the great ornithologist Lord Lilford was busy buying Dutch birds from the London bird market and leaving them in open cages around Lilford Park near Oundle. The first nest was discovered in the spring of 1889 and over the next five years, little owls bred so successfully that Lilford was able to claim, 'that I have now fully succeeded in establishing it as a Northamptonshire bird'.

I can only surmise that the weather was particularly mild in the first decade of the twentieth century because the spread of little owls was remarkably rapid. By 1910, the Edenbridge owls had extended into Sussex and Surrey and the Lilford ones into all the neighbouring counties. Twenty years later they were to be found in most parts of England and much of Wales. The expansion was accompanied by a wave of ignorance and hysterical prejudice: Waterton appreciated in 1842 that this owl was 'prized by the gardeners in Italy for its uncommon ability in destroying insects, snails, slugs, reptiles and mice', yet in 1909, they were imported to New Zealand specifically to control small birds that had become orchard pests. In England and Wales, gamekeepers were convinced they predated on game chicks and every gibbet had a little owl hanging from it.

Such was the controversy over the little owl that the British Trust for Ornithology commissioned a detailed survey of the bird's diet in 1936. Over eighteen months nearly two thousand five hundred food pellets from sites across the country were examined, which disclosed that fifty per cent of the diet consisted of insects, five per cent small birds, with the balance principally small rodents. Only two pellets contained the remains of a game-bird poult. They became protected under the 1954 Protection of Birds Act at about the time the population declined through habitat and food loss due to agricultural intensification and pesticides. The population today seems to have stabilised at around ten thousand pairs.

Perhaps the most famous little owl was Florence Nightingale's pet, Athena, which she took everywhere in her pocket. To her great distress, Athena died on the eve of Florence's departure for the Crimea. At Florence's instruction, Athena was stuffed and taken to her family home, Lea Hurst in Derbyshire. In 2004, when Lea Hurst and its contents were sold, the Florence Nightingale Museum at St Thomas's Hospital acquired the one-hundred-and-fifty-year-old owl and it now has pride of place there.

Doocots

Killing time between the morning flight and the afternoon tide one September, I drove from Lindisfarne, where I had gone for a few days wildfowling, along the Northumbria coast to the enchanting village of Embleton in the shadow of Dunstanburgh castle. Embleton is noted for its miles of sandy beaches and dunes, which in summer are covered in a profusion of wildflowers – bluebells, cowslips, burnet rose and bloody cranesbill. Next to the church is the old vicarage, built on the site of Embleton Tower, a medieval pele (fortified house), and in an adjacent field there is an early example of a conical, beehive-shaped, 'random rubble' dovecote.

The domestication of rock pigeons, *Columba Livia*, appears to have occurred in the eastern Mediterranean region between five and ten thousand years ago. The ancient Egyptian, Persian and Greek civilisations kept enormous pigeon houses; the rich, delicate flesh of the squabs was highly prized and the dung, used in tanning leather, dyeing cloth and as fertiliser, was extremely valuable. The culture of pigeon keeping spread across Europe with the Romans and they undoubtedly established *columbaria* during their occupation of Britain. Although pigeon keeping died out here after the collapse of the Empire, it remained widespread in manorial France where squab was much appreciated as a delicacy in early medieval cuisine. The Normans brought the art of managing *columbiers* to England and with it, the complicated feudal rights restricting the building of pigeon houses to the nobility, the Church and Crown officials.

Ownership of a pigeon or *culver* house was a very desirable perk in Great Britain, and one that was to increase in value over the next five centuries. They were simple to establish, easy to operate, productive in the first year, protected by law and, best of all, the pigeons fed initially at the expense of the serfs and, later, the landlord's tenants.

Pigeons can breed eight times from early March until late October and the primary purpose of a dovecote was to provide a source of luxury food. Squabs are ready to eat within four weeks, by which time they are almost as large as their parents and very tender, since their flying muscles have never been used. Those born at the beginning of Lent were kept as future breeding stock, but from Easter Sunday until the end of November, dovecote pigeons provided a constant supply of squabs but, once breeding stopped, the adult pigeons were rarely eaten during the following three months.

The household accounts of Dame Alice de Byrene, of Acton Manor in Suffolk, for example, record 1535 squabs eaten by a household of twenty people between April and November 1412, but no pigeon meat at all until the following April. Apart from providing food, the dung was scrupulously collected to be used in tanning or dyeing and as a fertiliser, as already mentioned: indeed, it was valued at over ten times that of other manures.

The first beehive-shaped, 'random rubble' pigeon houses were already being built in the twelfth century. Foundations of a significant number of these have been identified stretching from Devon to Lincolnshire. Design had become much more complex during the fifteenth and sixteenth centuries, reflecting both the social status of wealthy Tudor landowners and the increasing value of culver house pigeons.

Squabs were now being reared on a commercial scale; this was the age of banqueting and there was an enormous demand for the delicacy. For example, two thousand of them were required for Archbishop Neville's enthronement feast at Cawood Castle in 1465. More important still, incomes from pigeon farming rocketed when the saltpetre-rich dung became a vital component in the manufacture of gunpowder. Some of the bigger pigeon houses, containing perhaps as many as two thousand nesting boxes, even had armed guards to prevent thieves from stealing the dung. The consequences of harming domestic pigeons became increasingly draconian, with heavy fines, confinement in pillories for up to eight days, or lengthy prison terms; in Scotland, second offenders could lose their right hand.

The golden age of dovecote building was in the seventeenth and early eighteenth century, when pigeon houses proliferated across England and southern Scotland, particularly in the grain counties of Fife and the Lothians, with twenty-six thousand dovecotes recorded in England and an undisclosed number in Wales and Scotland. Follies were all the fashion and fully functional pigeon houses were disguised behind an incredible number of different architectural styles, many of which remain as listed buildings.

From the middle of the eighteenth century, pigeon farming went into a rapid decline as every section of farming was affected by the fever for improvement, fuelled by soaring food prices. The new spirit of energy and enterprise was driven by great landlords such as Townshend, Leicester, Egremont and Bedford in England, whilst Graham, Grant, Tweeddale and Hamilton led the way in Scotland.

Keeping pigeons at the expense of the tenantry was now considered extremely bad form, but when the Napoleonic Wars started in 1803, it was also seen as thoroughly unpatriotic. Available grain stocks were needed to feed the standing army as well as the general populace. Almost overnight, pigeon farming ceased, culver houses fell into disuse, squab disappeared from British cuisine and thousands of domestic rock doves became feral, seeking roosting sites in our towns and cities where they became classed as vermin.

Oddly enough, dovecotes are experiencing something of a rebirth; Pigeon Control Advisory Service International (PiCAS International) has piloted an urban 'birth control scheme', where feral pigeons are encouraged to breed in purpose-built dovecotes. Once laying starts, the eggs are replaced by dummies and PiCAS claim at least a fifty per cent reduction in the population, although it seems a missed opportunity not to let the eggs hatch and harvest the squabs…

An Autumn Fish

There is something utterly magical about fishing for an autumn salmon as the end of the season approaches: mist lies on the water in the early mornings, leaves are changing colour, there is still a hint of purple on the hills and scarlet berries hang on rowan trees. As the muggy, leaden days of summer draw to a close, bringing strong September winds and associated increased rainfall, river levels rise significantly. The scent of fresh water encourages salmon from around the coastal estuaries to swim inland to spawn in their natal rivers and there is no more exciting or magnificent sight than a glittering silver fish porpoising joyfully up river.

Tragically, the autumn run of fresh fish coming in to our rivers on every tide has dropped dramatically over the last four decades. The Atlantic Salmon Trust and their scientists are desperately working to identify the causes of this trend and reverse them, but back-end fishing, even for a gravid fish, can still be the highlight of the season.

With the breeding season approaching, the colour of the cock fish gradually changes to his autumn livery, particularly the gravid fish that has been in fresh water all summer. The skin thickens and becomes leathery, whilst the greater part of the flanks turns to a deep coppery red, with grey and yellow on the belly, giving him the soubriquet of 'soldier' up here in the Borders. As fat reserves will be low now, the arch of the back collapses and the body loses depth. The snout grows considerably longer and the lower jaw acquires a distinctive upturned hook or kype, which in some cases becomes so pronounced it protrudes above the corresponding recess in the upper jaw. This purely male characteristic seems to have no real function except perhaps as a visual deterrent to other males; it is useless as a weapon of attack or defence and prevents the jaw from closing. It is no use either in constructing the spawning redds amongst the gravel, as this is done exclusively by the hen fanning her tail. Whilst cock fish undergo a radical transformation, hens gradually become a dark grey colour with traces of purple and blue along their flanks and gill covers, remaining otherwise little altered except for a steady expansion of the abdomen as the spawning season progresses and their wombs fill with ova.

An entirely different set of tactics is required from the previous couple of months for back-end fishing: more than at any other time of the season, rods must be adaptable and prepared to adjust flies and lines to the fickle behaviour of fish or conditions which may change overnight. The early morning or late evening sorties armed with light gear, after fish in search of oxygen-rich fast runs or attempts to seduce the lazy ones trapped in pools with low warm water, are a thing of the past. A heavy fall of rain on parched ground up in the hills after a dry summer will cause a raging spate, and the associated drop in temperature causes a frenzy of activity, especially in pools where fish are lying in decent numbers. A rising spate is full of debris, river trash and possibly soil from early ploughing, but once this has cleared, fish will be in exuberant spirits, keen to move upstream. A falling spate is the perfect time to fish.

During the spawning migration up river, both cock and hen fish become aggressive and territorial, snapping at anything which intrudes. Unless you hit an unseasonal period of low water, you should expect to fish with a sinking line of a density determined by depth of water and power of flow. There are several options in types of line available nowadays and it really depends on personal preference and conditions on the day. A Skagit line is easy to cast if you are fishing from a boat, Spey lines are preferred by people who like a long-bellied line that does not need to be retrieved so far in before re-casting and a shooting head system is nice to handle and adaptable to most conditions. As with everything else connected with fly fishing, there are endless permutations: but the ultimate aim is to frustrate otherwise reluctant fish into an aggressive response, by invading their territory and getting a fly deeper and closer to them.

It goes without saying that if fish are going to see a fly in water stained by sediment, it needs to be coloured, with red, yellow and orange being particularly irresistible at this time of year. Among fishermen's tales there is the no-doubt apocryphal story of a rod sitting on the bank eating an orange and a fish striking a piece of the peel tossed into the water. There are plenty of modern flies to choose from: Big Red Francis, Super Snaelda Red and Gold copper tube or a Jock's Shrimp to name a few. All are good high-water autumn flies, but so too are some of the old, tried and tested traditional ones.

The Jock Scott, invented by and named after Lord John Scott's ghillie when he took the Makerstoun beat on the Tweed in 1850, is still a killing fly. No fly box is complete without the famous Willie Gunn, a hair-wing version of a Thunder and Lightning, named after the Countess of Sutherland's ghillie on the Brora. Originally intended for spring fish, it soon became recognised as the most successful hair-wing pattern ever tied for autumn salmon. Then there is the historic Collie Dog. I vividly remember my father in the rod room of the Oykel Bridge Hotel at the end of September back in the mid-1950s, holding up a fly with silver body, long black hair (now goat hair, but originally a sheepdog's), red throat and hackles, and saying, 'When all else fails, my boy, there is always the Collie Dog'.

Any fish caught are going to be released and rods will be using single hooks, much easier to extract than doubles or trebles. For a basic rule of thumb, water volumes determine the weight of fly: the bigger the water, the bigger the fly, and different tackle is needed for fish moving between pools after a spate. Fish tend to travel close to the bank, taking the easy route upstream by avoiding powerful flows in sometimes comparatively shallow water, where one might have stood to fish a few weeks previously; or they lie in sheltered resting spots off the main current at the tail of a pool, in smooth flows or beside a shelf in an incoming stream. They are very territorial in these often gravelly runs, where they use the up current to keep them steady; an intermediate line with sink tip to dangle a fly in front of them is ideal for this sort of water.

Small flies tied on a size 8 to 10 hook with colour and movement are good for stained, murky water – a Stinchar Stoat, perhaps with a gold body for a bit of sparkle, the ubiquitous Ally's Shrimp, an Aurora Cascade or an old favourite, the Garry Dog. For clearer water, try a silver-bodied Green Flee, a Yellow and Black Monkey or perhaps a Silver Stoat, early flies that have all done me well in the back-end and have activated the angry response one wants. On overcast days, the natural fluorescence in a fly with a bit of white in it, whether a traditional Jungle Cock or a modern copper-tube Black and White Snaelda dropped over a known salmon lie and moved slowly from side to side will invariably annoy a fish enough to trigger an attack reflex.

Back-end fishing quickly disappears. The season for Scottish rivers, such as the Borgie and Naver, Helmsdale, Spey, Shin, Oykel and Aberdeenshire Dee, the Southern Irish rivers and in England, the Dart and Exe, are among those that close on 30th September. More, such as the Brora, Ness, Tay and its tributaries in Scotland, the Tamar and Eden in England and most of the Welsh rivers, close on or about the middle of October. The vast majority of the rest close at the end of the month except the Annan and Irvine, which close on the 15th November and the Nith, Urr and mighty Tweed on the 30th. The Cornish rivers, the Fal, Looe, Camel and Fowey, all close on 15th December.

How best to organise some back-end fishing, if one doesn't already have a juicy invitation from some kindly owner of a stretch of water? Whether you are hoping to fish one of the big four or any of the smaller rivers throughout the UK and Ireland the online booking, advisory and information service FishPal is one place to start. FishPal has fishing available on hundreds of fisheries with two hundred thousand rod days through the season and plenty in the back-end to suit all budgets, with a network of ghillies, guides and river managers providing daily information on river levels, as well as what fish were caught when and where. They can offer to book guides, instructors, tackle hire, wheely boats for disabled fishermen, provide links to accommodation and rod alerts to tell you if fishing is available where you hope to go and there is always an expert contactable by telephone.

Where would I go if I had the choice? Somewhere on the North Tyne and preferably, the Haughton Castle Beat. Not only is the valley stunning in autumn, but the Tyne is now indubitably the best salmon river south of the Border and a quite remarkable conservation triumph, when one considers how dreadfully polluted it once was.

The Month of the Rut

There is always an atmosphere of primitive excitement and expectation about October. Nature seems to be tugging the last of summer's goodness and energy out of the land, drawing in its defences and preparing for the challenges of the months ahead. A brooding defiance resonates in the glorious colours at this time of year: the yellow of crab-apples, deep purple of sloes and damsons, scarlet of rowan berries and yew berries, deeper red of rosehips or hawthorn. Above all, it is the visual impact of leaves turning on deciduous trees – the golds, bronze, russets and ochre of oak, ash, sycamore, sweet and horse chestnut, alder, walnut, elm or beech – that makes this month so stunningly beautiful.

'A fresh October brings the pheasant' refers to the powerful equinoctial gusts of wind that can shake a great beech or oak tree like a terrier shakes a rat, bringing down a shower of beech mast or acorns on which pheasants love to feed. We can expect the first touch of frost now and the month is full of old lore forecasting the winter weather. 'If a deer's coat is grey in October, there will be a severe winter' is one of the gloomy prognostications: other warnings include blue hares changing to their winter pelage, rabbits carrying a lot of fat round their kidneys and birds stripping the last autumn berries. A fall of snow in October, on the other hand, apparently guarantees a mild January.

The first chill winds bring with them little charms of tiny goldcrests – the woodcock pilots – feeding on thistle heads. The first wave of woodcock, which the French so eloquently call 'queens of the woods' and whose plumage includes all the shades of autumn, yellow, black, chestnut, russet, citron, gold and copper, start arriving from northern Europe, flying under the hunter's moon. Woodcock are not only the finest-eating gamebird, they are the most fascinating and challenging. Shooting woodcock over a couple of spaniels was once described by Colonel Peter Hawker as 'the foxhunting of shooting'.

There is a massive movement of birdlife as more refugees arrive, escaping from sub-arctic temperatures. Noisy flocks of arctic thrushes – the fieldfare and the redwing – appear, driven south from Iceland and Scandinavia, making the wildfowler's heart beat in anticipation of hard weather following close behind. Our estuaries are full of every conceivable species of waterfowl: a multitude of golden, ringed and grey plover, greenshank and redshank, oystercatchers and bar-tailed godwits. There are herds of ghostly, crescent-shaped curlews, endless trips of dunlin and teal, flocks of moth-like lapwings, densely packed gaggles of little pale-fronted Brent geese, eider duck and shelduck, plus the great northern waterfowl, whooper swans, early Bewick's and the whitefront, pinkfooted greylag and barnacle geese. Flocks of Lapland and snow buntings, and large numbers of skylarks, woodlarks, meadow pipits and rock pipits haunt the marshes and shoreline. The exultant cacophony of birdsong when this great assembly greets the dawn is, for me, one of the great attractions of wildfowling.

Badgers are industrious now, clearing old bedding out of their setts and dragging in new as they prepare for winter. In areas where the brocks have not eaten them all, hedgehogs are earnestly carrying leaves, grass and moss into the dens in which they will eventually sleep the winter through. As soon as the temperature drops to 10°C amphibians and reptiles go into hibernation: frogs to the bottom of ponds, while toads, lizards, adders and grass snakes find habitat inside piles of stones or beneath logs. These can be caught out if, as so often happens, there are four or five days of unseasonably warm weather around St Luke's Day, the 18th, when, traditionally, oxen were not worked: 'On St Luke's Day, oxen have leave to play.' Midges reappear to dance in the sunlight, a few butterflies sleepily search for nectar and bats re-emerge at dusk. Such a period is known as 'St Luke's little summer'.

October is also the month of the rut. All summer our red stags have been preparing for this moment, growing new antlers to replace the ones cast in the spring and laying on 'grease' (fat). Now mature beasts, those over five years old, move on to the hinds' home ranges and gather a harem of twenty or so, which they defend by strutting, posturing, roaring and, if challenged by another mature beast, fighting. There is no more primitive sound or primeval sight than two of our largest mammals, coats matted and antlers dripping in peat mud, bellowing lust-crazed defiance at each other, whilst a group of hinds grazes quietly nearby. Stalking in the early part of the rut is at its most exciting and challenging; there are so many variables, with jittery eyes and ears shifting about all over the hill.

The clocks go back on the 28th and Halloween (or Hallowe'en) is on the 31st. This was the Celtic festival of Samhain, marking the end of the light (or growing) half of the year and the start of the dark (or dead) half. The Celts believed that the spirits of their ancestors now became active at nightfall. The early Christian church was quick to impose its own interpretation, creating All Saints' Day, also known as All Hallows' Day. The Canadian poet, Virna Sheard, links the two so vividly in her poem Halloween:

> *Hark! Hark to the wind! 'Tis the night, they say,*
> *When all souls come back from far away –*
> *The dead, forgotten this many a day!*

Hell Hounds

At the end of October, leaves darken and fall, trees become gaunt and lifeless; the landscape appears increasingly bleak, the earth gives off an ancient, musty smell and the uncanny calling of geese moving under a hunter's moon completes the picture of eerie starkness. These ghostly voices, similar to the distant sound of hounds in full cry, have been the source of myth, folklore and superstition since antiquity. These are the gods marshalling the spirits at Samhain, the Celtic celebration of the dead. Odin, of Anglo-Saxon legend, furiously thundering across the sky on his eight-legged steed with his ghastly pack of jet black, broad-headed, baying hounds. The Wild Hunt of the Middle Ages, with its following of cannibalistic hags, the moaning souls of hanged criminals and unbaptised children, all led by a horned huntsman and his fire-breathing hell-hounds.

Throughout history, the description of this spectral horde and its leader has undergone numerous changes and regional variations. In Cornwall, the licentious priest Dando, cursed for drinking with the Devil, hunts his hounds for all eternity. Gwyn ap Nudd, Lord of the Dead, whose hounds, unusually, are pure white with red ears and bellies, searches the skies of Wales for the souls of the recently deceased. Herne the Hunter, a reincarnation of the Celtic god Cernunnos, casts his hounds above Berkshire and Windsor Forest in particular, wearing the antlers and skin of a white hart. Satan himself reputedly kennels a pack among the ancient dwarf oaks and moss-covered boulders of Wistman's Wood on Dartmoor.

The hounds, individually or collectively, are known by many local names and, apart from in Wales, are all uniformly black. Yeth, Yell, Wisht or Heath hounds hunt the moors of the south-west for the souls of children who died before they were christened. In the north of England, Gabriel or corpse hounds and Gabble Ratchets howl across the moonlit sky, sometimes hovering over the house of someone about to die.

East Anglia has been terrorised by Old Shuck for centuries, a hell-hound 'huge and hideous' with 'eyes like saucers and horrible'. Sometimes the beast appears headless, floating on a carpet of swirling Fenland mist, particularly near bodies of water, graveyards and at crossroads where suicides were buried and gallows often sited. The most notable sighting of Old Shuck was on 4th August, 1577, when it suddenly appeared among the congregation of St Mary's Church at Bungay, in Suffolk: 'All down the church in midst of fire, the hellish monster flew. And, passing onward to the quire, he many people slew.' It then galloped off to Holy Trinity at Blythburgh, ten miles away, killing two people, injuring others and causing the steeple to collapse into the font.

Solitary black hounds crop up sporadically to terrorise mortals in other parts of the country. South Yorkshire has the Padfoot, which becomes the Barguest in the north of the county; Westmorland, the Capelthwaite; Lancashire has the Skriker; Somerset, the Gurt Dog; lowland Scotland, the Kirk Grim and in the Highlands, Cù Sith, a hound the size of a cow, with a bark loud enough to be heard by ships at sea. All of these – except Cù Sith, which specialises in abducting women – skulk round graveyards or remote highways and presage death to anyone who sees them.

There are any number of more credible legends of haunting by phantom hounds. Roslin Castle in Scotland has the spectre of a great war mastiff belonging to an English knight who was killed by the Scots at the Battle of Roslin in 1303, which howls for its master on stormy winter nights. Newgate Prison, that stood on the site of what is now the Old Bailey, was haunted by a black dog which appeared just before executions. It was first seen after a scholar, imprisoned on a charge of witchcraft, was killed and eaten by his starving fellow inmates. The battlements and corridors of Peel Castle on the Isle of Man were haunted by the Mauthe Doog, a black spaniel belonging to Simon, Bishop of Sodor and Man, who died in 1247. When his grave was opened during excavations in 1871, the skeleton of a dog was found at his feet.

Devon has more phantom hounds than any other county, including the hell-hounds of Squire Cabell. Richard Cabell of Buckfastleigh, on the edge of Dartmoor, lived in the 1600s and gained a reputation for being an evil and immoral man, who was believed to have murdered his wife and signed a pact with the Devil. He died in 1677 and on the night of his interment in Holy Trinity churchyard, a pack of ghost hounds came racing across the moor and howled round his grave until a shadow emerged and took them hunting. In an attempt to lay his soul to rest, the villagers placed a slab of stone over the grave and built a barred sepulchre above it. All to no avail: the hounds still come and bay for their hunting.

A more recent phantom dog is the bull terrier, whose stuffed head used to repose above the bar of The Star Inn in the Essex village of Ingatestone. In the first decade of the twentieth century, the landlord of The Star possessed a fighting bull terrier of unusual cunning and ferocity. When it became too old for the pit, it amused itself by savaging any dog unwittingly brought into the pub. Today, there are areas of the pub from which dogs will unaccountably bolt with their tails between their legs. Needless to say, during the passion for ghost stories and tales of horror, mystery and imagination of the nineteenth and early twentieth centuries, spectral hounds provided material for many authors.

An obvious example is *The Hound of the Baskervilles*, in which Arthur Conan Doyle combines the legends of Old Shuck with the story of Squire Cabell's hounds hunting across Dartmoor, to produce his Sherlock Holmes thriller. Dora Havers, writing under her pseudonym of Theo Gift, wrote *Dog or Demon*, the ghastly tale of the land agent for an Irish landlord, who evicts an old man from his cottage. The old man's dog is burnt to death and subsequently returns, charred and vengeful, to claim the life of the agent's newborn baby.

Quite the most thrilling and frightening ghost story about hounds I have ever read is *The Shadow on the Moor*, written by Alan Ian, eighth Duke of Northumberland. It is based in the 1820s in what is now the West Percy Hunt country and is centred around a huntsman, Black Tom Fletcher, who was notorious for both his skill with hounds and his furious temper. After one particular day's hunting, the whipper-in, Jim Murray, is brought back to kennels unconscious, having suffered terrible head injuries. Black Tom claims that Murray has fallen off his horse on the cobbled road, but just before he dies Murray regains consciousness long enough to tell his wife that Black Tom beat him over the head with his brass-handled whip for miscounting hounds. On the way back from the funeral, Murray's widow meets Black Tom. 'Driven and hunted ye shall be,' she curses him. 'Driven and hunted to your grave.'

On the next day's hunting a ghostly holler is heard. This is the voice of Jim Murray and, as hounds take off on a scent, a shadow appears although there are no clouds in the sky. Hounds hunt deeper into the hill country, drawn on and on by ghostly hollers, while the shadow follows behind. One by one the field drop off until only Black Tom and one other are still riding. As daylight fades, the shadow moves closer and hounds, Black Tom and the remaining member of the field are no longer hunting, they are being hunted, riding for their lives on floundering, blown mounts. Finally, the shadow reaches Black Tom and, with a dreadful shriek, he and his horse are swept over a precipice.

Sleep well this Hallowe'en.

Beautiful But Deadly

In early October AD 54, the Emperor Claudius sat down to a dish of his favourite mushrooms, the sweet-tasting and highly prized esculent *Amanita caesarea*, which had recently begun its autumnal appearance in the oak woodlands around Rome. Unknown to him, his wife Agrippa had instructed the poisoner, Locusta, to spike the ovoli with another mushroom of the same species – *Amanita phalloides*, the aptly named Death Cap. These innocuous-looking, pale yellow or greenish fungi, found globally in deciduous woodland during late summer and autumn, hold toxins that are among the most potent known to man.

Symptoms of poisoning by *A. phalloides* and the equally deadly *A. virosa* – a beautiful, pure white mushroom known as the Destroying Angel – are the same. Very little happens for six to twelve hours but then the victim is gripped by fierce abdominal cramps, insatiable thirst, nausea, vomiting and severe watery diarrhoea. This lasts for around twenty-four hours when, typically, there is a remission of symptoms. Unless the sufferer is alert to the cause of his discomfort, he begins to feel slightly better and assumes he is recovering from a nasty dose of gastroenteritis. Claudius, who was notorious for gluttony and intemperance, would simply have thought that he had been overdoing it a bit.

By now, devastating amatoxins are busy destroying cell tissue in the liver and kidneys. As necrosis in these vital organs prevents poison being filtered into the urine, the amatoxins become reabsorbed in the blood stream and recirculated, causing repeated liver and renal damage. Within a few days, the stomach cramps, vomiting and diarrhoea return, with agonising intensity. *A. phalloides* causes ninety per cent of the deaths from mushroom poisoning and, despite years of research, there is no known antidote. If diagnosed quickly enough, organ damage can be limited with dialysis and intravenous fluids, anti-emetics, activated charcoal to remove toxins from the gut, corticosteroids and drugs to alleviate muscular spasms. Lives have been saved by organ transplants but death in over thirty per cent of cases is caused by catastrophic liver and kidney failure.

There are remarkably few incidents of serious illness or death by mushroom poisoning in Britain, largely due to our national antipathy to fungi. Most tragedies occur in Europe and Asia where fungi are historically part of the food culture and in America, particularly among immigrant communities. This situation, however, is expected to change with the ever increasing interest in natural foods. Edible fungi are promoted as gourmet delicacies on television food programmes, in cookery books and lifestyle magazines, with mushroom foraging becoming a popular autumn pastime. The majority of the two thousand species of fungi common to most countries are harmless. Some are culinary treasures. Around fifty will make you extremely unwell and there are probably six that can be considered deadly including Death Cap, Destroying Angel and Spring Amanita (*A. verna*) – all of which can, to the uninitiated, resemble edible field or wood mushrooms.

Two of the other lethal types are *Cortinarius speciosissimus*, often found growing in moss among conifer trees, and the rare *C. orellanus*, sometimes seen in deciduous woodland. These medium-sized, ochre-coloured fungi are periodically mistaken, with appalling consequences, for the delicious chanterelle mushrooms so eagerly sought by foragers. As with *Amanita* poisoning, the initial symptoms of vomiting and diarrhoea, although unpleasant, can easily be misdiagnosed as non-life-threatening. Meanwhile, the *nephrotoxin orellanine* is hard at work on the kidneys, destroying cell tissue and causing terminal necrosis to the proximal tubules. The secondary symptoms, blinding headaches, extreme thirst, debilitating back pain and a constant urge to urinate, may take a fortnight to appear. The extent of renal damage during this latent period can only be treated by hemodialysis or a transplant.

The sixth type, which appears right at the end of winter, is *Gyromitra esculenta* or false morel. These brownish, convoluted, brain-like truffles found in sandy pinewoods emerge at the same time and look similar to the highly prized common morel. Unfortunately, false morels contain the very volatile toxin gyrometrin, which decomposes in the body into methyl hydrazine. This attacks blood cells, damages the liver and affects the central nervous system. Six to eight hours after ingestion the usual symptoms of gastroenteritis occur, with a bloated feeling as the liver swells. Dizziness, lethargy and exhaustion follow rapidly. Unless treatment to absorb poisons from the intestines and pryridoxine hydrochloride is quickly administered, the sufferer can die of convulsions and massive liver failure. Bizarrely, false morels are considered a delicacy in Scandinavia where they are boiled in several changes of water to remove the toxins. Even this is dangerous, as some of the gyrometrin evaporates as toxic fumes, meaning that adequate ventilation is essential.

A whole range of unpleasant toxins lurk in woods and old pasture at this time of year. Among those that should be avoided are all varieties of the small, nondescript, dun-coloured *Inocybe* mushroom, found in grassland and deciduous woodland. These contain varying degrees of the toxin muscarine, which causes profound activation of the peripheral nervous system. Symptoms, which are as startling to the afflicted as they are to anyone in close proximity – at a dinner party for example – occur within half an hour of ingestion. They are easily identified by vastly increased salivation, profuse sweating and facial spasms. Tear ducts overflow, pupils dilate and vision becomes blurred. Blood pressure drops, the heartbeat slows, breathing is laboured and there is an overpowering urge to urinate. Apart from those with a history of heart problems, who may be at risk of cardiac arrest, full recovery usually follows an intravenous injection of atropine.

Another species to be wary of is the *Coprinus* or ink cap. One variety, shaggy ink cap or lawyer's wig (*C. comatus*), which grows on lawns, garden rubbish heaps and along roadsides, is a delicious ingredient for stews and sauces if picked when the gills are still white. Its close cousin, common ink cap (*C. atramentarius*) – the medieval source of writing ink – found in clumps on similar habitat, is also very good to eat except that it contains the unusual toxin coprine. Coprine only becomes activated if the mushroom is consumed with alchohol, symptoms being identical to those produced by the drug antabuse (disulfiram), prescribed to alcoholics (with marginal success) in an attempt to discourage them from boozing. Within about ten minutes, the victim experiences hot flushes of the face and neck, an unpleasant metallic taste in the mouth, irregular heartbeat, a tingling sensation in the limbs and numb hands and feet. These alarming sensations are accompanied by the kind of migraine headache that inevitably leads to nausea and vomiting. Symptoms last as long as there is alcohol in the system.

It is the similarity between the edible and the dangerous that makes foraging for fungi so risky: one toxic mushroom that inadvertently finds its way into a basket of edible ones can contaminate the lot. Natural history societies provide excellent fungi foraging expeditions, with a mycologist on hand to provide identification.

One thing to avoid is putting any faith in traditional folklore when deciding whether or not a species is toxic. A poisonous mushroom will not turn silver black or cause milk to curdle. No amount of boiling will completely remove toxins nor will steeping in vinegar or brine. Wildlife are not dependable indicators either. Various small mammals nibble poisonous fungi with impunity and the digestive system of rabbits seems to be able to cope with *Amanita* and orellanine toxins, which led to the old remedy for patients *in extremis*. Based on the rationale that rabbit intestines must contain neutralising agents, they were force-fed chopped raw rabbit guts mixed with honey.

Hag Stones

An extraordinary amount of ephemera seems to have accumulated in my hall over the years. Old split-cane rods, gaffs and landing nets. Heavy, leather-cased military binoculars. Redundant hunting boots. Several tennis racquets in various stages of decay and a cricket bat signed by Colin Cowdrey. A ridiculous number of rams' horn crooks and walking sticks, some carved with the heads of horse, hound or terrier, others with blades for swatting thistles or digging out docks. In one of the corners, there is a quantity of World War II brass shell cases and beside them, a large, milky grey nodule of flint about a foot long and six inches deep. A fairly unremarkable lump of silica, one might think, except that it has a natural perforation from one side through to the other, which makes it very special.

The chances of stumbling across a stone with a hole through it – a flint turned up by a plough, a pebble on a beach or river bed – will probably only happen to most people once in a lifetime. Depending on composition, the perforation would have been created when the earth was hot or through the movement of water over many thousands of years. For early man living in the age of superstition, finding such a stone would be a momentous occasion. Stones in general had enormous significance but a hole through which one could see must have been the work of the most powerful magic.

Hag stones, witch stones or holy stones, were one of the earliest amulets against the supernatural and in parts of rural Europe are still believed to ward off the 'evil eye'. Even in my own childhood, country people hung hag stones, often passed from generation to generation, from their front door key or wore a small one on a leather lace round the neck. I remember our gardener had a tiny one attached by a silver ring to the fob chain of his pocket watch. It was common practice to suspend a hag stone on a red silk ribbon above a bedhead, to protect the sleeper from a nocturnal visit by 'the old hag'. This was the worst of all nightmares, when the victim experienced the terrifying sensation of being held immobile by a heavy weight pressing on their chest and the dreadful feeling of an alien presence close at hand. What is now recognised under the medical term 'hallucinatory sleep paralysis' left the sufferer drained and listless, and gave us the term 'haggard'.

Faith in the efficacy of hag stones as a defence against evil was universal from Scandinavia to the Far East, with different cultures attributing additional powers to them. To some peoples, looking at the full moon through the hole gave a sight into the hereafter. To others, they were a cure-all for most ailments and skin diseases in particular. A ship would not go to sea without one nailed to the mast and hag stones were also alleged to be able to control the weather. Their most widespread use was in protecting horses. An otherwise steady animal found sweat-sodden and exhausted in the morning was assumed to have been taken out of its stable and ridden overnight by some malign influence. A hag stone – the bigger the better – nailed above the stable door, or hung over a stall, was believed to act as a defence. The flint in my hall would once have been used for this purpose.

Horses were equally vulnerable by day. Their sudden sensitivity and unpredictable shying was interpreted as having been caused by the proximity of some malevolent force that only they could see. As a deterrent, small hag stones were stitched to the saddle and bridle. When horse trappings became more elaborate in Central Europe and the Middle East, hag stones were replaced by amulets of silver, brass or bronze, their surface polished to deflect the power of the evil eye.

Horse amulets have been found in ancient tombs across these regions of simple circular, star or crescent designs, representing the power of light over darkness. Historians believe horse amulets were brought to

Britain in the twelfth century by the Crusaders and enjoyed a brief period of popularity among the rich, before being suppressed by the clergy: the ancient, classic designs had clear connections to pagan sun worship and the Church was having none of it. That these survived at all is thanks to Romany gypsies, who continued to decorate their horse harness in the traditional way.

Horse brasses, as distinct from horse amulets, started to be seen in Britain during the agricultural revolution of the mid-eighteenth century. Improvers such as Coke of Holkham, Bakewell and the 6th Duke of Hamilton began importing heavy horse stallions from Flanders. Draft horses rapidly replaced oxen for farm work and these big, continental stallions were taken from village to village servicing local mares, their head collars decorated with polished brasses.

Early horse brasses were made in the same way as amulets had been for centuries, from hand-hammered sheets of brass called lattens. These were still made in the classic designs of antiquity and were cut, filed and hammered into the desired shape. Horse brasses from this period are extremely rare and of great value.

By the 1820s, demand for harness decorations, particularly for dray horses and tradesmen's drafts, exceeded the production capacity from hand-hammered brasses and specialist metal workers began making horse brasses in sand casts. Walsall became the centre of brass casting, with several small foundries producing horse brasses, buckles and harness fittings. This was the heyday of brass-making for harness ornamentation. The traditional designs remained ever popular, but increasingly, businesses and corporations had their own motifs made up; commemorative brasses came into fashion and heraldic devices were required for the carriage horse harness of the nobility and gentry. The trade sank into decline in the 1930s with Stanley Bros, who were established in 1832, remaining as the last horse-brass-maker still casting by hand.

The spectacular sight of heavy horses on parade, with every inch of harness covered in glittering brasses, has come a long way from a handful of stones stitched to a bridle. But hag stones have by no means been forgotten. They can be bought, just like everything else, on eBay.

The Cottager's Pig

Running the length of one side of the cellars under my farmhouse is a broad slab of slate, supported on substantial brick pillars, its surface scored with shallow grooves. This is the old 'salting table' on which hams and bacon flitches were cured, with the liquid drawn out of the meat by the salt dribbling down the grooves in the slate and into an open drain running through the cellar.

Until the 1960s, the slate would have been packed with meat at this time of year; fat bacon was the mainstay of the rural diet and the majority of farming families and farm workers fattened a pig every year. A piglet was purchased as a weaner in the early spring and fed on household scraps, waste from the vegetable garden and excess milk from the house cow. The fattening pig was nurtured until the beginning of November, by which time it would be fat enough to kill. Traditionally, the slaughter was carried out when the moon was on the wane, to allow the pig to put on an extra ounce or two grazing by moonlight.

I can just remember as a small child the excitement, frenetic activity and sense of community spirit attached to the pig killing. The local butcher would arrive in his Morris 8 van with his tools to stick the pig and, as it was stuck, Mrs Truman, our cook, would be on hand to catch the blood in glazed earthenware crocks and collect the intestines as it was gutted. The pig was hung to cool until the following day when all the people who worked on our farm and their wives packed into the kitchen to help. The carcase was scalded, scraped and butchered; everyone had a job and nothing was wasted. Pots bubbled as lard was rendered down, the head and trotters were simmered for brawn, trimmings chopped for pork pies and sausages. The tripes were cleaned, turned inside out and salted for sausage casings, while the blood from the sticking was mixed with oatmeal, chopped fat, suet and spices for black puddings.

There was a constant stream of people in and out of the cellar, carrying bellies, bacon and ham joints to the salting shelves and covering them with a mixture of brown sugar, salt, saltpetre, crushed peppercorns and juniper berries. The kitchen filled with steam, the soft meat – the liver, kidneys and sweetbreads – was fried up and vast quantities of home-brewed beer supplied to keep everyone going.

By then the death knell of the cottager's pig was already sounding and an immense change in the diet of rural Britain was created with its passing. Fifty per cent of the agricultural workforce left the land in the first two decades after World War II as machinery replaced manpower, and with them went many of the crafts and skills essential to the old infrastructure of village life. The self-supporting type of family farm disappeared as the government implemented a policy of massive land reclamation or intensified agricultural production, while the emergent supermarkets began to dictate the nation's eating habits. These stipulated a standardised pig breed that was lean, fast-growing and tasteless. To conform to market demand, commercial pig farmers were obliged to farm supermarket pigs exclusively and many regional breeds, such as the Cumberland, Lincolnshire Curly Coat and Dorset Gold Tip, became extinct.

I used to keep a fattener every year and apart from ensuring I had a constant source of bacon and a decent ham at Christmas, there is something enormously soothing about watching a pig eat. The interminable guzzling has a hypnotic effect, so brilliantly illustrated by P.G. Wodehouse in his portrayal of the Empress of Blandings, Lord Emsworth's fat pig in the Blandings Castle novels. A couple of years ago, I conceived the idea that, as an alternative to chemical sprays, pigs could be used to eradicate bracken on the farm by grubbing down and eating the rhizomes, the invasive, carbohydrate-rich root system. I electric-fenced some weaners on to a big bank of bracken out on the hill and throughout the summer the experiment was a huge success; the weaners thrived on the rhizomes and I would go so far as to say my bracken-eradicating pigs were the sensation of the district. Unfortunately, just as I was about to bring them home in early November, we had an unexpected heavy fall of snow. The pigs all escaped over the electric fencing, taking up residence in the wood behind the farmhouse and predating spectacularly into the garden at night until the snow melted and they could be captured.

After this episode, it seemed politic not to keep pigs for a bit, but then you don't need to keep a pig to make your own bacon. A handful of dedicated pig farmers maintained a nucleus of some of our indigenous breeds and with consumer demand for choice and the growth of Q Guild butchers, farmers' markets and other fine food outlets, pork from breeds such as the Tamworth, Berkshire, Gloucestershire Old Spots and British Saddleback is now easily accessible. Curing bacon is simple; there are plenty of recipes available and all that is required is a piece of belly pork, and some salt and sugar, and twenty-eight days later you will have bacon that bears no resemblance to the insipid pink slices sold in plastic packets, which glisten with chemicals and exude grey scummy liquid when cooked.

Sporrans

On a half-landing of the main staircase in my grandparents' house there hung a life-size portrait of my great-grandfather, Colonel David Price Haig, wearing the full dress uniform of the Cameron Highlanders, complete with campaign medals, scarlet doublet, kilt and scarf plaid in Erracht tartan, dirk, broadsword and enormous, grey, goat-hair sporran. As children, my sister and I were terrified of this imposing moustachioed figure, whose ferocious gaze stared directly at us as we hurried past. But it was the goat-hair sporran, with its deep, heavy, cast gilt cantle and six gold tassels, suspended by blue and gold twisted cords, about which we wove our childhood fantasies. It was so vast and hairy, covering the whole front of the kilt and cascading down below its hem that we persuaded ourselves the sporran was capable of sprouting horns and leaping from the frame to chase us through the house. My sister spoilt the sporran game one wet afternoon when we had been happily frightening ourselves, by pointing out that great-grandfather would look pretty silly if he wasn't wearing it. Indeed, 'no truer word was spoke' – for without a sporran, Scotland's national dress is little different from a sarong.

Sporrans have their origins in the simple pouch attached to a belt, made from a circle of leather with holes punched round the periphery and drawn together with a thong, which must have been worn since before biblical times. In the Middle Ages, these pouches were referred to as 'scrips' – for example one twelfth century reference to Highlanders describes them as 'barelegged, wearing shaggy cloaks and a scrip'. The shaggy cloak was the *breacan-an-feileadh*, a belted plaid that became known as the great kilt, a loose garment of coarse checked cloth about five-and-a-half yards long and three metres wide. Part of the plaid was secured round the waist by a belt, with the surplus arranged over the shoulders as a cloak. At night it served as a blanket. The scrip or sporran, often made of deer skin and worn at the side, was used to hold valuables such as money, or flint and steel, whilst other things, such as food, were carried in the voluminous folds of the plaid.

The kilt as we know it today is said to have been invented in 1725 by an Englishman, Thomas Rawlinson, who managed an iron smelting works at Invergarry in the Great Glen. Rawlinson became increasingly frustrated at the inconvenience to his workmen and lost man-hours caused by the loose top half of the belted plaid and insisted it be cut in half. This idea was taken up by Ian MacDonell, Chief of Glengarry and the little kilt, the *feileadh-beag*, gradually replaced the belted plaid, with the sporran now hanging at the front. As more lairds took to the small kilt, sporrans became made of seal skin and quarry species such as otter, badger, wild cat or pine marten, as well as deer or calf skin, with silver cantles engraved with Celtic or heraldic design.

Except for existing Scottish regiments, the tartan and any form of Highland dress was banned under the Dress Act of 1746, after the Jacobite Rebellion had been crushed at the Battle of Culloden. Offenders were liable to six months' imprisonment for the first offence and transportation for seven years on the second, but this was the age of the Scottish Enlightenment and a growing humanitarian reaction to the plight of impoverished Highlanders, with deep concern that the historic culture of an ethnic people was about to be lost. The Highland Society of London, founded in 1778, was largely responsible for the Dress Act being repealed on 1ˢᵗ July 1782 by the Act of Abolition and, from that date on, Highlanders were 'no longer bound down to wear the unmanly dress of the Lowlander'.

Scottish Romanticism was by now well under way, fuelled by the writings of poets and authors such as Hume, Smith, Macpherson, Burns and, in particular, Walter Scott. Several Highland regiments were raised in the last decades of the eighteenth century, among them the Seaforths, Argylls, Sutherlands and Gordons, whose bravery, battle honours and martial bearing in their kilts, scarlet doublets, feather bonnets and enormous, tasselled goat or horse hair *sporran moloch* made them the pride of the British Army.

For some time, Highland lairds had been forming societies in Edinburgh, Aberdeen and other centres, including London, to discuss land improvements, the preservation of Gaelic culture and to promote the 'general use of the ancient Highland dress'. Such was the swell of interest in Scotland that in 1822, ministers proposed that King George IV should visit Edinburgh and Scott seized the opportunity to organise an elaborate, week-long, plaided pageant. Ancient Scotland would be reborn and George, his corpulent figure swathed in full Highland dress, complete with plumed headdress and goat hair *sporran moloch*, presented as the new Jacobite King. The *pièce de résistance* of the royal visit was to be a Grand Ball, an event which all Scottish society aspired to attend; but the proviso set by the King, that unless in uniform, 'no Gentleman is to be allowed to appear in anything but the ancient Highland costume', had Lowland lairds and wealthy merchants frantically searching for Highland ancestry. This led to a sudden demand for dress sporrans and tartan cloth, and is considered the moment when what had previously been perceived as the primitive garb of a remote and isolated minority became the national dress of the whole of Scotland.

Hitherto, Highland tartans had simply been patterned cloth associated with regions or districts, produced by local weavers using the natural dyes available in those areas. After King George's visit, followed by Queen Victoria's purchase of Balmoral in 1848 and her obsession with anything Scottish, Britain was swept by the 'tartan craze'. Woollen mills and cloth manufacturers were now swamped with orders to create tartan cloth artificially associated to Highland clans from those wishing to claim Scottish heritage. It was boom time for the mills and kilt makers; the rail network pressed north to Inverness and wealthy Victorians scrambled to emulate royalty by acquiring Highland estates and thereby claim some connection to a Scottish ancestry.

Chemical dyes and the Victorian penchant for ordered taxonomy gave cloth merchants an open field in designing faux historic tartans in unlikely colours within the different types – hunting, dress, chief's, Royal or mourning. No less busy were taxidermists and sporran-makers, struggling to meet the demand for an endless variety of sporrans to suit the kilt styles. These included plain, tanned calf skin day sporrans with folding flaps, with or without leather tassles; semi-dress sporrans in leather with a fur, deer or seal skin front panel and corresponding tassles; or badger, otter, pine marten and wild cat (the clan badge of the MacPhersons), with the masks fashioned to form the flap; dress sporrans in different furs, with heavy, elaborately designed silver cantles; and the massive regimental *sporran moloch*, with multiple tassles in goat or horse hair.

The tartan craze is in no way diminished, in fact if anything it is on the increase with sporran-makers here and overseas as busy as ever before. One Scottish sporran-maker told me that apart from their annual turnover of civilian sporrans, when the Royal Scots Borderers, Highland Fusiliers, Black Watch, Argyll and Sutherland Highlanders and the Highlanders (Cameron, Seaforth and Gordon) were amalgamated to form the Royal Regiment of Scotland in 2004, he received an order for five thousand horsehair full dress sporrans and five thousand regimental day sporrans. Forty per cent of their output is exported, including a considerable quantity of horsehair sporrans made for pipe bands all over the world.

There is nothing like an old sporran, preferably handed down from generation to generation, but where would one go to buy a new one? Janet Eagleton – who was awarded the MBE for sporran-making in 2001 – and her son, Marcus, of Scottish Sporrans, make handcrafted sporrans at their workshop in Perthshire, which can be custom-made to civilian or military customers' own specification. The Eagletons have a diverse client list including HRH Prince Charles, the actor Samuel L. Jackson and Super Bowl champion (but Scottish-born) Lawrence

Tynes, for whom Marcus fashioned a sporran out of the match ball from the 2008 Super Bowl final.

Jennifer Cantwell, of Sporran Nation in Forres, creates limited edition, bespoke and personalised sporrans with a modern edge, using different shapes, colours and unusual materials. Amongst her favourites are salmon skin and copper, giving a Scottish tradition a contemporary twist. Jennifer has designed sporrans to commissions from the actors Alan Cumming and Kevin McKidd, film director Mark Andrews, comedian Keith Lemon, rock star Lenny Kravitz and cyclist Sir Chris Hoy.

Using skills learnt from a taxidermist near Oban, Kate McPherson of Wild Sporrans, near Beauly, specialises in traditional skin sporrans, with clients from as far afield as America, Hong Kong, Singapore, Australia and even The Falklands. Apart from sporrans in red, roe, sika and fallow deerskin, Kate has made them from species as diverse as woodcock, mallard, polecat, brown or blue hare and pheasant, as well as from exotic safari trophies, such as genet cat, buffalo, impala and springbok. She is often commissioned to make 'firsts' from among British game species – grouse are popular – but will happily make a sporran from any skin, provided its acquisition falls within current wildlife legislation.

Kate produces a number of badger sporrans annually, all from road kill: and to keep in step with the law she must receive a letter from the person who finds a dead badger, fully explaining its cause of death. To make a sporran from pine martens or red squirrels, Kate first requires a licence from Scottish Natural Heritage, but alas, no matter the circumstances of a wildcat or otter's death, it is illegal to use their skin. I asked Kate what her favourite was. 'Mink is beautiful to work with,' she told me. 'But fox is always fun. You can make the mask so expressive.'

What does the modern Scotsman carry in his sporran? The short answer is 'as little as possible', particularly if he intends to swing a nifty leg at the Skye or Oban Balls. Realistically, once the sporran started to be worn over the groin, any weight precluded energetic activity and a mobile phone, or even a car key, becomes an offensive weapon when bouncing to the *pas de deux*. As a receptacle, the sporran is spectacularly useless, but then again, the kilt would look pretty silly without it.

Winter

Tracks in the Snow

It was not the red alert warnings of snow and high winds on the BBC weather map, nor the forecaster describing the effect of a fast approaching Arctic thrust meeting the temperate high pressure system we had enjoyed for the previous week, that convinced me a blizzard was on its way. Nor was it the unhealthy yellow tinge to the sky and the dirty grey, black-streaked nimbostratus clouds banking up to the north ('when clouds look like black smoke, a wise man puts on his cloak'). It was the behaviour of the hefted hill ewes out on the moor that was the clincher.

As dawn breaks, hill sheep work their way down from the high ground, where they have spent the night, to graze in the valley bottoms; in the afternoon, they move back up to the high ground. This is known as their 'rake', and they do it every single day regardless of the weather – except when they sense a blizzard is on its way. On the afternoon in question, as the wind began to gust, they were all sticking to the low ground like glue. The snow flurries began about an hour later, with the main force of the storm coming as the light faded.

All night it raged and thundered round the house, lashing against the windows in fury and thumping against the doors, but by dawn the massive energy had worn itself out, leaving utter silence and the eerie stillness of exhaustion. I love a good snowstorm; it is not just the pristine whiteness of an altered landscape that thrills, there is no better medium than soft, fresh snow for revealing the dramatic story of wildlife, so quickly and so obviously. The tracks the animals leave make a fascinating study: a whole episode of day or night movements, with their tales of tragedy or escape between predator and prey, are writ large for us to unravel.

The high wind had blown the snow into great drifts against any north-facing obstacle, but elsewhere it lay in a gentle covering and when I came out of the house soon after daybreak, the yard was already criss-crossed with little tracks. The evening before I had spilt a bucket of meal coming out of the feed store and once the free-ranging bantams had scratched away the snow, all manner of song birds – robins, thrushes, blackbirds and a variety of little tits – had flown over and hopped or skipped around it, leaving a circle of their different sized, three forward and one heel toe footprints. Mice had been scuttling along the side of the old steading wall to the same food source and leaving odd little tracks like a cloven hoof but distinguishable by the faint drag marks of their tails. Easier to recognise were the palm, three splayed fingers and short thumb of the forefoot of a rat and the long sole of his hind foot.

The footprints of a grey squirrel were clearly visible among the oak, ash and Scots pines in the wood behind the steading. Because of the animal's bounding motion on the ground, a squirrel's hind feet always land ahead of the front and having bare soles (unlike a stoat or fox), their toes and pads are very distinctive in snow. Its forefoot shows only four toes, since a squirrel has a fleshy lump instead of a 'thumb', whilst the hind foot shows five, with the three middle ones of equal length. Squirrels only come down from trees for a purpose and this one had travelled fast, with distances between bounds of a yard or more, until it slowed and hopped to a particular spot where it had dug through the snow and leaf mould to retrieve a buried hazelnut.

On the edge of the wood where the moorland fringe starts, there was an imprint where a cock pheasant had left his roost in a big ash tree but landed clumsily, with a clear impression of his outspread wings and the fan of his tail feathers. The track of a pheasant in snow is recognisable by three fore toes and absence of the heel toe, which being higher than the rest leaves a barely discernible mark. I was able to follow his meandering progress along the side of the wood, passing various places where he had stopped to scratch for seeds; as we approached the corner above the Liddel Water, his tracks were joined by those of a fox. The pads of a fox are narrower and more compact than those of a dog and when trotting or, in this case, stalking, his hind feet are placed exactly into the print of his forefeet, forming a single-file track. I could see the mark of his brush as he crouched ready to spring and the deep imprints as he stood on hind legs to leap; the tell-tale disruption in the snow; then a scattering of feathers; and finally his tracks moving on alone, with the drag marks of his prey.

Walking along the steep bank above the Liddel Water, where hazel and willow grow, I noted a depression in the bracken where a roe had lain up and the delicate slot marks leading away from it. Slimmer and more pointed than those of a sheep, deer are 'straight line' walkers like a fox, placing the hind foot in the print of the forefoot. In snow, the marks of the dew claws become visible. The toes of the slot of a buck are larger than a doe's and bucks walk more evenly and have a deeper 'trace' than a doe; the toes are closed if they are moving fast, becoming widespread as they tire or the ground becomes soft.

At the bottom of the bank beside the river were the large splayed prints of a heron, with the very visible heel toe and further along, running parallel with the water, an unmistakable 'slide' where an otter had crossed the ground from one bend in the river to another. In mud, the 'seal' of an otter is recognisable by the webbing between the five toes, the round ball they have under the sole of their pad in place of a heel and the distinctive mark in the mud left by their pole or rudder, as the tail is called. In snow their track is a continual smear with the deeper imprints where they have propelled themselves along with their hind legs and occasionally, disturbed areas where they have stopped to roll. Otters, like dogs, love the sensation of rolling in fresh snow.

Similar to an otter's slide is the track of a badger. On the side of a sheltered cleugh above the river we have an active sett, where the badgers are very industrious at this time of year, pushing out old bedding and hauling in bracken litter to replace it in preparation for cubs being born in a few weeks' time. In wet weather, the marks of a badger are identifiable by the five long claws of his powerful broad forefeet, which he uses for digging, and the narrower, long-heeled hind feet: but in soft snow his track is simply the wide drag mark where he has bulldozed his low slung body along, stopping periodically to dig for worms and beetle larvae.

On the moorland edge, where clumps of reeds grow profusely, the snow was laced with tiny vole tracks and lines of little depressions where it had collapsed behind them as they burrowed below the surface. I passed the tracks of the fox on his way down to the wood and an orange urine stain where he had paused to mark his territory. He was moving slower here, leaving scuff marks as his pads dragged through the snow with each step and, in places, I could see the soft imprint of his nose where he had stopped to sniff for food under the snow.

There were plenty of grouse tracks higher up where the heather showed through the snow; smaller than a pheasant's, they show no heel toe either. Further on a raven had been feeding on the carcase of a blue hare, leaving large, three-toed footprints with the long heel toe round the carcase. Among his prints were the similar but smaller ones of crows, which would have come in to feed once he had finished. Back towards the steading I passed a south facing slope riddled with rabbit burrows and among the network of tracks leading from them, the elegant, rounded prints of a hunting stoat. The prints of a rabbit and a hare are similar, with the hare's being larger; the hind legs leave a long, narrow print – the entire shin touches the ground – while the forefeet leave an oval mark. When running, the fore prints are close together with the hind parallel to them but when hopping or sitting the fore prints are in front.

The following day, the temperature rose, the snow seeped away in flood and all these secrets disappeared.

Red Letter Day

The Christmas holidays of 1961 started inauspiciously. I arrived home to find a different pony in the place of my old, beloved, grey gelding and a new head girl in charge of the stables. Between them, these two created a considerable collapse of confidence in me: the head girl looked fierce and the Connemara mare was enormous compared to the old grey. Worse than both of these things, though, was the mare's name. No thirteen-year-old boy should be forced to ride a pony called Trudi.

The first morning, I rode the Connemara on exercise and she seemed from my perspective to be a hell of a 'puller'. Afterwards I was made to put her over some jumps, under the critical eye of my father and the head girl. Father, an ex-cavalryman and something of a martinet, made it clear that my efforts fell short and unless matters improved, my inadequacies would be ironed out by the head girl over the holidays. The acid test was to be a day with the Old Surrey and Burstow on the coming Saturday.

I was a picture of woe at the meet and, if anything, cheery banter from Jack Champion, the legendary huntsman of the OS&B, about the new pony looking the right sort, lowered my spirits further. It was a warm, poor scenting day and the morning was spent with the field mooching pleasantly from covert to covert whilst I wrestled with the hard-mouthed brute, closely scrutinised by the head girl.

Scent mended when the temperature dropped and hounds were quick onto a fox. Not long afterwards, I got left behind trying to shut a gate with a broken hinge. By the time I remounted, the field had disappeared and the sense of relief at escaping the head girl was soon replaced by anxiety at the consequences of getting lost. I hacked on for half an hour and then in the distance saw Jack taking hounds across a paddock and into a wood. Following seemed to be the most sensible thing to do and I soon found the post and rails where he had jumped. It was only a small place and I put the Connemara at it, nearly going over her neck when she refused. Time and time again I tried to get her to jump; I clearly remember howling at her at one point: 'Do you really want to spend the entire holidays going round and round the schooling yard?' But it was no good.

Weeping with mortification, I rode back across the paddock and hacked sadly along a tarmac road. A car follower told me where the field were and in due course I saw nemesis in a top hat trotting towards me. 'Just been talking to Jack,' Father said. He knows, I thought bitterly; and as only a thirteen-year-old in the depths of misery can, decided that from now on I would never ride anything other than a bicycle ever again. 'Seems to think the world of you,' he continued, to my enormous astonishment. 'Told me you tried to follow him over a dam' great obstacle and when the pony wouldn't have it, used language he hadn't heard since he was a trooper in the Life Guards during the war. Says you're a regular little jockey and can whip-in to him any time, but not on that pony.'

Jack Champion was a great man in many different ways, but to have accurately interpreted my predicament and then taken the trouble to put things right with my father, was an act of kindness I have never forgotten. It is entirely due to him that I have since had so many red-letter hunting days. And Trudi? Replaced the following week by an old-fashioned grey cob called The Badger.

Christmas Week

'O dirty December, for Christmas remember.' (Thomas Tusser, 1524-1580) Of all the months in the year, December is my favourite. I love the bleak beauty of gaunt, leafless trees, the barren, lifeless landscape and ancient, musty smell of decay. December to me is the glorious colours of a cock pheasant glinting in thin winter sunshine as it rockets out of cover; the music of hounds in full cry; and the eerie sound of a great multitude of geese rising from their shore roost in a lapis lazuli dawn.

We should expect a hard frost with the full moon at the beginning of the month and an influx of little plump waxwings from Northern Europe and Scandinavia. A 'waxwing warning' presages a band of freezing weather, when an irruption of these noisy birds with red tips to their wings and distinctive crests arrives, stripping the last autumn berries. Waxwings, also known as snow birds or 'Bohemian chatterers', from their wheezing, crackling, clicking and stuttering calls as flocks of them, occasionally numbering many thousands, frenetically work the hedgerows or invade urban parks and gardens.

The ghostly sound of tawny owls calling to each other is one that is synonymous with freezing December moonlit nights: to quote *Love's Labour's Lost*, 'Then nightly sings the staring owl, Tu whit; Tu who'. These two sounds are not made by a single bird but are the contact calls of a male and female, as the cock bird begins his courtship feeding, bringing food for the larger hen in the hope of building her up for early breeding.

There is an almost tangible sense of brooding expectancy lying across the land at this time of year, as nature senses a change in the season.

The hours of daylight are at their shortest now, with temperatures lowest and for the next four months until spring, the battle for survival among wildlife is at its most severe. The hibernants are snug in their hibernacular, but everything else – deer, rabbits, hares, shrews, mice, voles, for example, and most birds – struggle by on body fat stored over the summer and autumn glut and what little they can find through the lean winter months. Predators, meanwhile, reap the benefit of their prey's weakened condition. The longest night is on 21st December and the dawn of the winter solstice, with its imperceptibly lengthening hours of daylight, gives hope to animals and humans alike. This day has been celebrated by mankind for many millennia, since well before the birth of Christ.

The early Church was very clever at converting the heathen population of these islands to Christianity by gradually superimposing an appropriate Christian celebration, such as a saint's day, on top of the many pagan seasonal festivals. In time, the principal twelve-day celebration of light over darkness, which began with the winter solstice and was known as Saturnalia in southern Europe and Yule in the north, became the festival of Christ's nativity. In western culture the Feast of St Thomas occurs on 21st December, but until the calendar reforms of Pope Gregory XIII were adopted by Britain in 1752, the winter solstice fell on 13th December, St Lucy's Day. The start of the Christmas festivities was an occasion for great celebration, with bonfires, dancing, merry-making and children chanting 'Lucy light, Lucy light, the shortest day and the longest night', until silenced with buns flavoured with saffron, known as Lucy's Eyes.

St Lucy was well qualified for such an important occasion in the pagan calendar. She is one of eight women, including the Virgin Mary, who are commemorated in the Canon of the Mass; her name is derived from the Roman *lux*, meaning light, and the manner of her martyrdom was particularly grisly and impressive. Born to great beauty, wealth and privilege in Syracuse about 283 AD, she underwent a religious conversion during the Diocletian persecution of Christians in 304 AD, dedicating her virginity to God and distributing her dowry to the poor and needy. Needless to say, this enraged the young man to whom she had been betrothed. He denounced her to Paschasius, the Governor of Syracuse, who ordered her to recant; but when she refused, he sentenced her to be defiled in a brothel frequented by Roman soldiers. At this she plucked out her eyes to avoid the lustful stares of the clientele, which is why she is depicted in high Renaissance art by painters such as Domenico Beccafumi (1486-1551), holding a plate on which her eyes have been tastefully arranged. After many vicissitudes, she was placed on an enormous and furiously burning bonfire from which she emerged unscathed, finally succumbing to a blow from a sword only after she had received the Sacrament.

The sound I always listen for on frosty, moonlit nights during Christmas week, when I take the terriers for their nightly run down towards the ruined castle where Mary, Queen of Scots hurried to succour her wounded lover Bothwell, is the unearthly shriek of a vixen. Near the top of the Castle Brae, the hill rising above the castle, is an earth among the jumbled boulders that are all that remain of the great wall which once surrounded the castle's deer park. When I hear the vixen screaming that joyous, urgent summons across the valley, I see her in my mind's eye, running backwards and forwards in the moonlight on the flat rock above the wall, ears cocked, listening as the answering barks of the dog fox come ever closer. This primeval mating call in the depths of bleak mid-winter, with its promise of spring birth, warmth and regrowth, is the real message of Christmas.

Christ's Animals at Christmas

A colony of bees lived in the roof of my parents' old home. Probably they were descendants of those once kept in hives in the alcoves along the south face of the walled garden. This colony had been in the roof so long that the tiles below their entry hole were stained black. A Christmas Eve tradition when my sister and I were children was to be taken up into the attics of the house just before bedtime. Tiptoeing by torch light, past ghostly piles of leather trunks and old furniture hanging with cobwebs, we would go to where we could hear a faint murmuring behind the panelling that covered the eaves. This, we were assured, was the bees – God's little servants – joyously humming Psalm 100. This convinced us of the truth of folklore's belief that animals were granted the power of speech on Christmas Eve and that they knelt in memory of those that attended the nativity at Bethlehem.

There are any number of myths and legends connecting animals to the twelve days of Christmas and, like the festival itself, many have their origins in pagan animal cults, sacrifices and fertility rites, such as the Roman festival of Saturnalia and the Yule celebrations of northern Europe. The winter solstice, with its lack of growth and sunlight, was a time of deep anxiety and fearful superstition for early pastoral communities. The old year was dying and the gods must be persuaded to start the new one. As we have seen, early Christianity often appropriated pagan traditions, reinventing them using their own interpretations, and much of our animal folklore stems from the religious fervour and pious anticipation of that period.

Other beliefs are more recent and the product of nineteenth century romanticism by popular writers such as Sir Walter Scott, Charles Dickens and Washington Irving.

The fifth century Christian poet, Aurelius Prudentius Clemens, is credited with the idea of giving animals human voices, enabling them to join the angels in adulation at the arrival of the Messiah. This notion seems to have been a relatively short-lived one, lasting only until 1223, when St Francis of Assisi received permission from the Pontiff to use live animals to recreate the nativity of Jesus for the benefit of the inhabitants of Grecio. As the popularity of nativity plays spread across Europe, folklore credited God with granting animals of the stable the ability to speak for an hour at midnight on Christmas Eve. In Eastern European countries it is considered very bad luck to catch them at it, as they often predicted the death of their masters. This predicament was avoided in Britain, where the myth was conveniently altered so that animals would never make use of their gift if they could be seen by humans.

Myths surrounding donkeys would have come from their prominent role in nativity plays. Christian tradition differs over whether the previously unmarked hide of a donkey received its dark, cross-shaped mark for providing the transport that got a heavily pregnant Mary as far as Bethlehem, or for carrying Jesus into Jerusalem. Either way, dark hairs taken from the cross were worn well into the nineteenth century in charms, to heal ailments which ranged from toothache to fits. Passing a child three times under and over a donkey was believed to cure whooping cough. Sometimes the hairs were mixed with bread and eaten or, alternatively, a complaint could be passed on to the donkey by putting a lock of the sufferer's hair in the animal's feed. A black donkey was believed to prevent mares from miscarrying and for some bizarre reason, to stumble across a dead donkey was considered the best possible luck.

Much folklore also grew up around the robin, whose inquisitiveness always made it appear a friend of people. Robins are associated with modern Christmas more than any other bird. They are most visible in midwinter, as food shortage makes them tame and they puff out their feathers against the cold. In legend, robins acquired their colouring when one punctured its breast trying to pluck thorns from Christ's head at the Crucifixion. Early Christian mythology has a robin rescuing St Leonorius, a sixth century Welsh missionary to heathen Brittany, from starvation, whilst a dead robin gave St Kentigern, founder of Glasgow Cathedral, the opportunity to demonstrate his saintliness by bringing it back to life. Acts of kindness by robins became the focus of several eighteenth century poets, among them Wordsworth, Thompson, Blake and Percy, who described a robin covering the abandoned children with leaves and moss in the tragic ballad 'The Children in the Wood', better known as 'The Babes in the Wood'.

Robins and wrens are often linked in mythology – 'the robin and the wren, God's cock and hen' – but the wren's lineage is much more ancient. Wrens were Druidic birds of prophecy and have always been protected by a superstition of dire consequences to anyone who harmed one. Contradictorily, one of the oldest and elaborate folk rituals, once widespread in Britain and still surviving in Ireland and parts of Europe, was the St Stephen's Day Wren hunt. On 26th December, groups of youths armed with sticks, known as 'libbetts', would beat hedgerows until a wren was caught and killed. This was hung from the top of an elaborately decorated pole and paraded to every house in the locality, where a feather would be plucked and given to the householder as a protection against witches.

The origins of this primitive custom are very obscure. The most widely held belief is that a wren alerted the guards when St Stephen was attempting to escape imprisonment, causing the death of the first English martyr. However, the Wren cult appears to have been brought to Britain by prehistoric traders during the Bronze Age and to have its ancestry in Saturnalia, Ancient Rome's most important fertility festival. During the week-long orgy, starting on 17th December, the roles of master and slave were reversed, moral restrictions removed and rules of etiquette ignored. Wrens were the king of birds in Greek mythology and killing one at this time of year represented the end of the old season and the start of the new one.

A dove was depicted in early Christian literature as the manifestation of the Holy Spirit at Christ's baptism and has maintained its position through the centuries as the emblem of peace. Ravens, although they fed Elijah and featured prominently in Celtic mythology, have failed to last the course, except in Wales, where a belief persisted that a blind person who fed ravens would regain their sight. Eagles have been a symbol of power since time immemorial and there are frequent references to them in the bible. An eagle was the beast of Revelations assigned to St John the Apostle, which is why the lectern in virtually every church in Britain is carved in their shape. An exception is St Andrew's Church at Boynton in Yorkshire, where the lectern is carved in the shape of a turkey, with the bible supported on its outstretched tail feathers.

William Strickland, a gentleman adventurer who sailed with Sebastian Cabot to South America in 1526, is considered to be the first person to introduce turkeys to Britain. Strickland made a fortune from several voyages to the New World and bought estates at Boynton and Wintringham in 1542. He was granted arms in 1550 and took as his crest 'a turkey-cock in his prime proper', liberally adorning the church at Boynton with his armorial. Turkeys remained an exotic addition to feasts until the mid-eighteenth century, when George II developed a passion for eating the bird; an area of Richmond Park was sectioned off specifically for rearing them. Their popularity grew and by the end of the Victorian era, turkeys had become synonymous with Christmas. Every autumn, vast flocks of turkeys, their feet hardened with tar, were walked from farms in East Anglia, where they had been fattened on post-harvest gleanings, to poultry markets in London.

Turkeys replaced goose or beef as the centrepiece of the Christmas feast, they in turn having been the substitute for boar's head. It is surprising that so little mythology remains about the boar, a creature of such iconic status in legends across Europe and the Middle East. Boars were an emblem of war and destruction; divine figures on standards, coins and altars; the quarry of heroes; the transport of Gods; the most significant fertility symbol and the most powerful of the Yule sacrifices. A decorated boar's head, carried into the dining room with much pomp and ceremony, was the highlight of Christmas banquets throughout the Middle Ages.

One of the earliest carols, published by Wykynd de Worde in 1521, is the 'Song of the Boar's Head'. The ritual of serving a boar's head on Christmas Day continued until the religious festivals of Whitsun, Easter and Christmas were banned by Parliament, during the Puritan purges of Cromwell's Commonwealth. The custom survives with the annual Boar's Head Feast at Queen's College, Oxford, but for most of us the last echo of the pagan boar cult is the tradition of buying a ham at Christmas.

Belief in a benign deity riding the winter skies, dispensing reward or punishment, stems from pagan worship of the god Odin. As ever, Christianity adopted the idea and in the fourth century, St Nicholas was introduced, a saint renowned for his generosity to children and the poor. Different cultures across Europe created their own interpretations of a mystical bringer of gifts to good children at Christmas. These manifestations came at night, flying through the air on horseback or in a carriage drawn by goats or dogs.

The contemporary conception of St Nicholas in the form of jolly, fat Santa Claus, in a sleigh drawn by reindeer, has been accredited to Clement Clarke Moore, a professor of Oriental Studies at Columbia University in New York. In 1822, Moore wrote the poem, 'The Night Before Christmas', based around the Christmas folklore of northern European immigrants in New York and his knowledge of reindeer cults in Lapland and Siberia. Nomadic Sami tribesmen had a tradition of gathering hallucinogenic fly agaric toadstool and feeding it to their reindeer. The reindeer's digestive system removes any poisons, leaving hallucinogens intact in its urine. Drinking the urine induced an effect similar to LSD and stoned Samis imagined, amongst other things, that reindeer could fly. Moore's vision became widespread with the gradual commercialisation of Christmas, particularly after 1930 when Coca-Cola used the image of Santa Claus in an advertisement.

Artists always portray Santa's reindeer with full sets of antlers. At a dinner party not long ago, someone posed the question as to what sex Moore intended them to be. The bulls lose their antlers after the rut in October; oxen – castrated bulls – which the Lapps (Samis) use as draught animals, in March; and the cows, after they calve in the spring. Before I could explain all this, a formidable woman on my right announced authoritatively that the reindeer were female. Asked how she was so sure, she replied, witheringly: 'Silly man would get lost otherwise, wouldn't he?'

Mistletoe

O f all the essentials that make a Christmas – the tree and the holly, turkey, Bradenham ham, sirloin of beef, plum pudding and mince pies – none is more fundamental yet easily forgotten in the last-minute flap than mistletoe. To my mind, Christmas is not Christmas without the dowdy little sprig of angular twigs, with their pale green leaves and milky-white berries, pinned above the door of my drawing-room.

It is not so much that mistletoe means old fellows like me might get the occasional kiss, nor the plant's ancient association with the Roman festival of Saturnalia and its significance to the Druids, that makes it so essential at this time of year. It is more what the rare sighting of mistletoe must have represented to superstitious early man. A Neolithic herdsman, perhaps – trudging home in the dead of winter – believing all plant life had ceased and suddenly seeing a green clump of growth with leaves and berries glowing in a shaft of sunlight, high in the bare branches of an oak tree. This would be a startling assurance that the ritual bonfires and human sacrifices were doing their stuff; that spring really would come again, bringing warmth, fecundity and new life.

Mistletoe is, by any standards, one of nature's most remarkable phenomena: a hemiparasite, of which there are thirteen hundred species and sub-species worldwide, they use trees and shrubs as hosts, joining to them by an intimate xylem system called a haustorium. Mistletoes use the host plant as a growing platform and a source of water and nutrients, relying on the chlorophyll in their leaves to manufacture food through photosynthesis. All are found growing above ground, except for one species exclusive to Western Australia, which appears to be a freestanding shrub, but whose root system taps in to those of every neighbouring plant. *Viscum album* is the only species in Britain, found colonising soft-barked deciduous trees south of the Humber, especially apple, but also hawthorn, blackthorn, lime, poplar, maple, willow, plum, rowan, crab apple and, occasionally, oak.

Mistletoe growing on an oak was the Golden Bough of Celtic legend and was held in great reverence by the Druids. In February and March, tight clusters of small, yellowish-green flowers appear which, from a distance, look like a patch of golden mist in a crook between the branches. Pollination is carried out by flies feeding on mistletoe nectar and the green summer berries produced by the female plant turn white and sticky in November, ripening towards the end of December and into January. At one time a resinous concoction made from mistletoe was painted on branches to trap birds.

Mistletoe is distributed haphazardly by birds with the main vectors of seeds being mistle thrushes – hence the name – and increasingly, as our climate changes, by overwintering blackcaps, particularly in the Severn Valley. Mistle thrushes (*Turdus viscivorus*) disperse seed by excreting the still sticky seeds and blackcaps (*Sylvia atricapilla*), rather more efficiently, through eating the fruit and wiping their beaks free of the seed on the branch of a tree. Mistletoe can be germinated artificially by smearing ripe, sticky berries on the bark of a branch at least twenty millimetres in diameter in early February. Attempts to reintroduce mistletoe to London are part of several boroughs' biodiversity conservation schemes and trials are currently being monitored on selected trees at the Chelsea Physic Garden, Holland Park, Enfield Lock and the Haringey Railway Fields Nature Reserve.

Although mistletoe has a symbolic significance to the winter solstice going back into the mists of time, any pagan association was frowned on by the Church and the plant only gained national popularity as a Christmas decoration during the Victorian era. This was fortuitous for apple growers. In the nineteenth century, Britain had over fifty thousand hectares of orchards in Kent, the West Midlands and Somerset, providing the ideal habitat for mistletoe. Mistletoe reduces the yield of its host and the metre-high spherical clumps increase the risk of wind-blow in a storm. To protect their trees, growers would cut mistletoe in late winter and early spring, once the toxic berries had died back, and feed it to the sheep grazing the orchards. As the Christmas market for mistletoe expanded, harvesting during the first three weeks of December became the traditional method of control, with the mistletoe sold in auctions at Tenbury Wells in Worcestershire or at Covent Garden; sellers with bundles of mistletoe were a common sight in Victorian London. An increase in demand and the gradual decline of our own apple orchards led to mistletoe being imported from France, Germany and Spain.

If it took a long time for mistletoe to find a niche as a Christmas decoration, apothecaries and herbalists since Pliny had been convinced that so unusual a plant must contain powerful medicinal properties. A phoenix holding a mistletoe berry in its beak was a mediaeval apothecary's sign. The dried leaves, small twigs and flowers, collected just before the berries formed and made into a tincture, were prescribed for sterility and any nervous disorder that resisted other remedies. Sir John Colbatch, the great eighteenth century surgeon and physician, was determined that: '...there must be something extraordinary about that uncommon beautiful plant, that the Almighty had designed it for further use than barely to feed thrushes or to be hung up superstitiously.' Colbatch experimented extensively but inconclusively on using mistletoe to cure epilepsy. The search for a successful pharmaceutical use for the plant continued throughout the nineteenth century, particularly in Europe.

In the 1920s, the Austrian philosopher and educationalist, Dr Rudolf Steiner, created anthroposophic medicine, developing ideas about the healing properties of certain plant species that could be linked to specific ailments. As a parasite, mistletoe was associated with cancer. Steiner's theories brought mistletoe into the era of modern scientific research and led to the foundation of the Society for Cancer Research in Switzerland.

His suggestions for developing special extracts into a sterile solution which could be injected and his advice for mistletoe treatments have since been substantially developed in Germany and Switzerland. Extracts of mistletoe are now widely believed to inhibit tumour growths and to stimulate the immune system. There are, however, considerable differences in extract quality, depending on the season and the host plant. Despite this, mistletoe remedies have a devoted following – the Germans spend over thirty million euros annually on a wide range of preparations – and clinical research is ongoing.

The Holly and the Ivy

N ot one symbol of Christmas is more associated with the spirit of goodwill, peace and joy, than holly, with its shiny, dark green, spiky leaves and brilliant, blood-red berries. Holly is everywhere at Christmas; it is sung about in carols such as The Holly and the Ivy, or Christmastide Comes in Like a Bride 'with holly and ivy clad'. It is the principal illustration on thousands of Christmas cards; the centrepiece of wreaths; it decorates homes; and no flaming Christmas plum pudding is properly dressed without a sprig of berried holly browning in the flames.

Since the 1850s, when the Victorians created Christmas as we know it today, tons of holly have been auctioned annually at the famous Tenbury Wells Holly and Mistletoe auction in Worcestershire. Tenbury Wells sits beside the River Teme, where the counties of Shropshire, Worcestershire and Herefordshire meet, in an area particularly suited to the growing of holly. For a hundred and fifty years the holly and mistletoe sales took place in the old cattle market, but are now held on three separate dates from the end of November at the Burford House Garden Centre, by auctioneer Nick Champion of Champion's.

There are many species of holly, of which the most common is European Holly, *Ilex aquifolium*, found from western Asia across Europe, Britain and Scandinavia. It usually grows as a shrub or small tree in hedgerows or the understorey of deciduous woodland, although it can form dense thickets or groves as the dominant species, growing up to fifty feet in height over a period of several hundred years. Holly is dioecious, meaning that male and female flowers occur on different trees. The female is pollinated by bees and other insects, such as the holly blue butterfly and various moths, including the yellow-barred brindle, double-striped pug and holly tortrix. The berries, which ripen in November, provide winter food for a variety of birds, among them thrushes, blackbirds, jays, robins and arctic migrants such as redwings, waxwings and fieldfares; the deep leaf provides habitat for hibernants. In the late eighteenth century, botanists discovered that the berries were produced exclusively by female rather than male plants, thus debunking much of the previously accepted folklore associated with the males of the species.

The leaves of holly were once a very valuable winter stock feed, particularly across the moorland of the north Midlands, with holly groves deliberately planted and preserved for that purpose.

The name 'holly' derives from the Anglo-Saxon *holegn*, and a grove of holly trees became known as a 'hag of hollins', with the word preserved in hundreds of place names, such as Holinsend near Sheffield, Hollingworth in Cheshire, or Hollin Busk and Hollin Edge Height near Bolsterstone in Yorkshire. The spikes on holly leaves gradually disappear as the tree grows taller and hollins were pollarded, with the branches fed to stock. Farm rents were adjusted upwards depending on the number of trees in the hag. Feeding holly was gradually phased out with the introduction of turnips during the Agricultural Revolution and one of the few remaining ancient hollin hags is near Snailbeach in Shropshire.

Holly had been revered long before Christianity, as a crucial element in the pagan mid-winter solstice celebrations, the most prolonged and widespread fertility festival worshipping the Unconquered Sun. To early people such as the Iron Age Celts, dreading the barren bleakness of winter, the sight of a holly tree, standing lush, green and aglow with scarlet berries when all other plant life had died, would have been an emblem of hope and a promise from the deities of regrowth to come. The fact that holly most commonly grows in the understorey of oak woodlands, where few plants can survive the overhang of a mature tree, added to the mystique. Oaks were sacred to the Druids for being the hosts to mistletoe, the Golden Bough, and they believed that once the leaves fell from an oak, its spirit moved to the holly growing nearby.

The first recorded decorative usage of holly was by the Romans during Saturnalia, the week-long celebrations held in mid-December to honour the agricultural deity, Saturn. It was a time described by the poet Catullus as 'the best of days', when all the accepted codes of conduct were reversed: men dressed as women and masters as servants. There were pageants, licentious plays orchestrated by a Lord of Misrule, uninhibited banqueting, bonfires, drunkenness and abandoned dancing; houses and streets were decorated with holly, ivy and other evergreens. Also *strenae* – twigs of evergreens, mostly laurel or holly to which were fastened sweetmeats – were given as gifts.

The early Christian converts continued to decorate their houses with holly and evergreens over this period, as much out of previous habit as for protection from persecution during the revels. The custom persisted as Christianity spread, despite stark warnings in the fourth century from Archbishop Gregory of Constantinople and an attempt to ban the practice altogether in AD 572, by Bishop Martin of Braga. Common sense had prevailed by AD 595 when Pope Gregory sent a mission of forty monks, led by Augustine, the Prior of the Abbey of St Anthony in Rome and later the first Archbishop of Canterbury, to England with instructions to convert the pagan inhabitants to Christianity. Pope Gregory's mandate to Augustine was brilliant in its simplicity: he surmised, accurately, that the easy-going Saxon population would not object if the seasonal festivals of the pagan calendar were Christianised, as long as no one interfered with the actual celebrations.

Conversion through gradual coercion took several centuries, but eventually Saturnalia – or Yule, as it was known to the Saxons – became the celebration of Christ's birth, with the traditional winter solstice woodland decorations remaining unaltered. Because of its significance to pagan beliefs, holly became more Christianised than any other plant; the Church claimed that the red berries represented Christ's blood at the Crucifixion and the spiky leaves, the crown of thorns. This notion became so ingrained in the psyche of early people that holly became known as Christ's Thorn or Holy Tree, the name William Turner MD, the Elizabethan natural historian, gives in his book *A New Herball* of 1551.

Less credible were the suggestions that holly originally shed its leaves in winter like any other tree, but when the Holy Family were fleeing Herod's soldiers, they hid in the dense foliage of a holly tree which was rewarded by keeping its leaves all year round. Essentially, from the perspective of the early converts, the traditional use of holly, ivy and other winter evergreens was not eliminated, as a rather cryptic entry in the ancient calendar of the Church of Rome suggests: '*Templa Exornantur*' – churches are decked.

During the Medieval period, Christmas remained a time of feasting and merrymaking; it was predominantly a secular celebration with a few token religious elements thrown in to keep the Church happy. The antiquary John Stow gives a description of Christmas in the fifteenth and sixteenth centuries in his work *A Survey of London* (1598): 'In the feast of Christmas, there was in the King's house, wheresoever he was lodged a lord of misrule, or master of merry disport, and the like had ye in the house of every nobleman of honour or good worship, were he spiritual or temporal.' Stow records that every man's house, the parish churches, the conduits where the people of London drew water and the boundary standards of the different wards, were decked with holly, ivy and bay leaves.

Church warden accounts from the early sixteenth century for the churches of St Laurence in Reading, St Mary-at-Hill in Billingsgate and St Martin Outwich in the City, all show expenditure for holly and ivy at Christmas. Amusingly, the Church of St Margaret, in the grounds of Westminster Abbey, was still defiantly being decorated with winter evergreens in 1647, the year Christmas was banned by ordinance of the Puritan Parliament as 'a popish festival with no biblical justification'.

Song was an important part of pagan winter solstice festivals and these were to become semi-religious ballads (the origin of our Christmas carols), in which a curious relationship between the holly tree and the ivy plant appears to have been a popular topic. Common Ivy, *Hedera helix*, was held in high esteem by early people; it was dedicated to Bacchus, the Roman god of drunkenness, and its leaves, either bound round the brow or added to wine, were believed to prevent intoxication. Ivy was an emblem of fidelity and for that reason, Greek priests always presented newly-weds with a wreath of ivy after the marriage ceremony. From the early Middle Ages, right up to the Interregnum when Christmas was banned, any number of ballads, poems and love songs were written about the two plants. Henry VIII even wrote one alluding to his love for a 'lady true' enduring, in the same way holly and ivy retain their evergreen vibrancy despite the harshest winter. Singing contests between men and women were a popular Christmas pastime, with men extolling the virtues of the 'masculine' qualities of holly, whilst women praised the 'feminine' qualities of ivy. One of the earliest examples, dating from the fourteenth century, is among the Harleian Collection of manuscripts in the British Library. Everyone's favourite Christmas carol, *The Holly and the Ivy*, probably dates from this period.

The belief that plants with winter berries, like holly, ivy and yew, were a defence against a malign presence, was particularly strong in Scotland. The Gaelic name for holly, *Chuillin*, appears across the country from *Cruach-doire-cuilean* on Mull, where the MacLeans of Duart adopted holly as their clan badge, to Loch a' Chuillin in Ross-shire in the north. The town of Cullen in Banffshire may also have derived its name from a local holly wood.

In old Scottish myths, the *Cailleach*, a hag representing winter, was said to be born each year at the beginning of November. She spent her time stalking the earth during the winter time, smiting the ground with her staff to harden it and kill off growth, whilst calling down the snow. On May-Eve, the turning point of the Celtic year from winter to summer, she threw her staff under a holly tree and turned into a stone. The holly tree was sacred to her and keeping a holly bough, complete with leaves and berries, in the house was believed to placate her and protect the occupants from her unwelcome visit.

After the battle of Dunbar in 1650, when Cromwell defeated the Scottish army commanded by Lord Newark, five thousand prisoners were force-marched under appalling conditions to Norfolk to drain the fens. The fourteen hundred Scotsmen who survived the starvation and ill-treatment on the journey south were said to have stuck twigs of holly around the hovels they lived in on the marshes, as protection against evil fen spirits.

Holly was believed to frighten off witches and also protect the home from being struck by lightning, with many old houses such as ours north of the Border having a holly tree growing close to the building. Curiously enough, these properties were first mentioned by the Roman naturalist Pliny the Elder (AD 23-AD 79), who further believed that the tiny white flowers which blossom in May, caused water to freeze and that a piece of holly wood thrown at any animal compelled it immediately to lie down beside it.

Although the berries are toxic to humans, holly leaves contain laxatine and ilicin, and were once used to treat rheumatic fever, whilst the bark was boiled by bird catchers to make bird lime. The wood is hard, compact and even-grained throughout, with a beautiful colour similar to old ivory. It is much priced by stick dressers, in marquetry and as a substitute for ebony when dyed black. Because of the ancient belief that the wood had a mystical power over animals, coachmen traditionally had whips made from coppiced holly which accounted for thousands of holly stems during the great era of carriage driving. There was a custom in the eighteenth and nineteenth centuries that coachmen were always buried with their holly whip.

Carving the Festive Bird

S ad to think that in many households across the country, much of the happy anticipation associated with Christmas luncheon will evaporate as soon as paterfamilias picks up his carving knife and attempts to dismantle the festive bird. In all probability this will have lain unused for the past twelve months and even the jolliest family gathering can be enveloped in gloom by the anxious efforts of a carver at work with a blunt knife. Not so long ago, when it was common practice among most families to buy a joint of meat at the weekend and eat Sunday lunch together, there was someone in every household proficient in carving. It was a necessary skill, passed from generation to generation and with a noble and ancient history.

At a time when the main food source was derived from everything that swam, ran or flew, the art of carving was elevated to become part of the code of chivalry, with a language as complicated as that of venery or hawking. Each and every species of fur, fish or fowl had to be carved according to rigid individual specifications based on their standing in the laws of hunting. Peacock were disfigured, herons dismembered, mallards unbraced, cranes displayed and swans, lifted. Plovers were minced, bitterns unjointed, woodcock, pigeon and smaller birds were thighed, whilst partridge and quail were winged.

There were at least twenty ways of carving fish; pike were splatted, barbels tusked, eels traunsened, sturgeon traunched and porpoises, under-traunched. Birds were not to be lifted by the legs, venison must not be touched by either hand and only the left used for beef or mutton. The exact spot to begin carving a roast was governed by elaborate rules, with slices from the larger beasts presented on a broad-bladed serving carver, cut into four bite-sized pieces held together by the fatty top strap. This was held in the hand whilst the pieces were chewed off and then thrown to the dogs.

A thorough knowledge of carving was considered so important that before the golden spurs of knighthood could be granted, a period of novitiate had to be spent as a carving esquire. Carvers in Royal and noble households tended to be aristocrats of lesser rank; a knight carved for a baron, a baron for an earl, an earl for a marquis and so on. The Earls of Denbigh and Desmond are the Hereditary Grand Carvers of England and the Anstruthers of that Ilk, the heritable Master Carvers to the Royal Household of Scotland. Such was the social gravitas attached to carving, that *The Boke of Kervynge* was published in 1500 by Wykynd de Worde, for the benefit of upwardly mobile Tudors, at a time when few books were being printed at all.

Raising the art of carving to being part of the code of chivalry was an expression of gratitude for food on the table and the same is true of the workmanship in making carving knives. During the Middle Ages, cutlers were craftsmen of similar stature to jewellers, master armourers and illuminators; they fashioned knives with handles of polished bone, horn, wood or brass, delicately inlaid with silver and gold or set with agate, amber or lapis lazuli.

The cutler's art thrived during the following three centuries, when banquets became increasingly elaborate and magnificent. Implements of great beauty were created as new and exotic materials became available – ivory, rock crystal, cornelian, mother of pearl, coral or silver set with niello. Some of these have survived in museums or exhibitions of the art and evolution of cutlery, to give an inkling of the pageantry of eating, when joints reigned supreme and 'made' dishes were never considered to be a main course. Cutlers made less elaborate but more elegant carving knives during the nineteenth century and it became customary for every newly married couple to have a boxed set as the centrepiece of their display of wedding gifts. This tradition persisted until eating habits changed, the weekend joint became largely a thing of the past and the art of carving was gradually lost to a whole generation. It is now very difficult to find anything remotely similar to the craftsmanship that existed when carving was at least a weekly occurrence in most households and Sheffield was world-famous for producing quality knives.

There is, of course, any number of high quality chef's knives available using the latest technology stainless or carbon steel, but these are essentially kitchen knives and ought not to be brought into the dining room. A carvery of knives, the correct term for a set of carving knives, should consist of two knives, one with a blade of about eight inches and an inch and a half in depth for large joints of meat and the bigger birds like turkeys or geese. The other, for small joints and game birds, duck and chickens, should be around six inches long and an inch deep. The blades of both must be slightly rounded as they rise to the point, for working into thigh joints. The set should also include a steel and a carving fork.

It may interest students of history to know that until the early seventeenth century, forks were unheard of in Britain, either for carving or eating. Joints were anchored by a smaller knife or skewer and it was the carver's job to see that slices of meat were presented in manageable pieces; thereafter the fingers or a spoon were used. Thomas Coryat, the son of a West Country squire, is credited with introducing forks on his return to Great Britain from a tour of Italy, where they had been in use for some time. Initially, neither Coryat nor his fork were well received; he was lampooned on the stage as a 'Furcifer' (from the Latin: fork-bearer or rascal), a nickname which stuck, and was condemned from the pulpit for suggesting 'that God's good gifts were unfit to be touched by human hands'. However, Jacobean England was becoming more sophisticated and the fashion for elaborate lace cuffs dictated a change in eating habits. Forks were soon in common usage, except in the Royal Navy, where they were considered effeminate until well into the eighteenth century.

Because so many of them were still in use until the 1960s, carvery sets of old Sheffield steel knives in good condition, many of them a hundred years old or more, can still be found on bric-a-brac stalls, in antique shops or on eBay. Anyone wishing to buy a set should look for knives with a depth of an inch to an inch and a half, depending on blade-length, that still retain a straight cutting edge and with handles that firmly fit the blade. A set in this condition will have bags of life left in it and if the soft Sheffield steel is discoloured, it can easily be brought back by rubbing with a paste made from ordinary baking soda moistened with water, vinegar or lemon juice. If water is used, be sure to wrap the blades in blotting paper after wiping dry to remove any remaining moisture; if vinegar, simply wipe clean and rub dry.

Knives like these were made for the dining room, in the days when they were expected to be in frequent use. They were intended to look impressive, but great care would have been taken in their balance and the way the antler or polished bone handles fitted into the hand. They will be infinitely more pleasant and appropriate to use than any modern equivalent.

There is no point in even attempting to carve unless one's knives are properly sharpened. Modern carbon steel or stainless steel knives have sharp, factory ground blades which will hold their edge indefinitely. Unless you know how to use a whetstone, an old set of Sheffield steel knives discovered in an attic or bought from an antique shop will require professional sharpening. Here your friendly butcher will almost certainly oblige, particularly if he thinks you will be buying joints from him in the future; he will sharpen your knives on the electronic grinding stone which every butcher has in his shop.

Once the knives are sharpened, the edge is maintained by using the steel. Many people are put off attempting this, having seen the almost acrobatic dexterity with which chefs or butchers use one. Butchers in particular are cutting meat all day, every day, and are not maintaining the edge on their knives, they are sharpening them with an entirely different steel to the one in a carvery. A butcher's steel is heavily serrated whilst a carvery one is virtually smooth – its purpose is simply to straighten the edge of a knife which is already very sharp. Maintaining the edge of a carving knife is actually simplicity itself. Take the steel in the left hand and place the point on the edge of a table. Hold the steel horizontally, i.e. level with the top of the table; place your knife on the steel with the two handles almost touching and the sharp edge of the knife facing away from you. With the knife at right-angles to the steel, turn the blade to an angle of about twenty-five degrees and stroke it along the steel in a half circle, keeping the two handles close together. This covers the whole length of the blade in one smooth action. Repeat a couple of times, then turn the blade over and start the process again from the point of the steel back towards you. Assuming the knife has not previously been blunted, it is now ready to use.

There are a number of ways of preserving the edge of your knife during carving. Never apply undue pressure, for this compacts the meat fibres, alters the shape of the joint, creates uneven slices and will ultimately blunt the knife. Let the knife do the work for you: it should be weightless in the hand and the whole length of the blade used, in long, even strokes. Be aware of when the knife's edge is about to come into contact with bone; when carving roast beef, for example, make an incision along the rib bone every so often to allow slices to fall free as you reach that point. Always use a wooden carving board when carving a rolled boneless joint, as nothing ruins a good knife quicker than coming into contact with metal or porcelain. When you have finished carving, wipe the knives clean with a damp cloth, dry them, rub the blades with olive oil and wrap them up in greaseproof paper. Never wash them in soapy water; this causes rust where the shank joins the handle and the knife will eventually break.

The Twelve Days of Christmas are traditionally a time of open-handed hospitality, when unforeseen guests could arrive at any time and if the young are still at home, there may be a sudden escalation of hungry mouths demanding to be fed. We have found the simplest and most economical way of coping with the catering is by having a selection of cold joints always on hand: a massive fore rib of beef, a Bradenham ham, a large piece of spiced beef and a variety of game. In many ways, these are as much a symbol of Christmas as the decorations, the tree and the mistletoe. A challenge for a novice carver perhaps, but always remember the carver's mantra: 'If your knife is sharp, the meat properly cooked and you keep your head, you cannot go far wrong.'

Dogs at Christmas

For most of us, Christmas week is a period of frantic activity, inducing energy and stress levels which are, according to statisticians, equivalent to moving house, planning a wedding or getting divorced. Similar extremes of emotion are involved: anxiety and frustration, euphoria and despair.

Life is no less stressful for our faithful and long-suffering hounds. The dark unease of shortening days is still felt, but the winter solstice creates imperceptible changes in the season that always unsettles them. Now sheepdogs fret because they work less. Gundogs fret because they work more. Lap dogs drop their tails at the late hours and unexpected commotion in the house. With their sensitive antennae picking up a range of conflicting human passions, is it any wonder that they become fractious and depressed?

One dog who suffers more than most from the Christmas malaise is Tug, my elderly terrier. An old-fashioned working type standing twelve inches at the shoulder, he was bred out of a bitch from the David Davies Hunt and a dog owned by the terrier man at the College Valley and North Northumberland Foxhounds. Predominantly white, he has a broad, flat skull, brown ears and thin black lines running back from the corner of each expressionless, obsidian, black eye, giving him a faintly oriental look. Somewhere in the mists of his impeccable genealogy, a Staffordshire bull terrier was crossed into the line to correct muzzle width and improve jaw. Although straight-legged and narrow in the chest, this addition to the breeding has given him massively muscled hindquarters and the rolling gait of a crocodile. Utterly fearless, single-minded and belligerent, Tug has become a legend in his own lifetime. In hunting circles he is known as 'Dyno-Rod'.

Tug is our only house dog and lives in a box lined with old shooting socks under a table in the gun room. When his services are not required elsewhere, he sees his role in life as guardian of my property, a responsibility fulfilled with the utmost diligence. His is a simple philosophy. If it moves, bite it. If it doesn't, piss on it. Every morning he sets forth on a menacing, stiff-legged tour of the farm buildings and garden, pausing every few yards to cock his leg as a warning to would-be intruders. Part of the circuit takes him past the sheepdog kennels and his 'Australian good morning' sets the whole lot roaring with fury. Satisfied that all is well, the rest of the day is spent in ceaseless vigilance, only relieved by the sense of achievement that comes from obliterating any strange scent with his own fresh pungency.

Christmas disturbs the smooth running of Tug's world and reduces him to the canine equivalent of dry, racking sobs. He is not the least bothered by the vagaries of human emotions as shopping fever mounts. What concerns him is the intrusion of alien smells that pollute his domain. In the days immediately before Christmas, armfuls of holly and a large Norwegian spruce redolent with woodland scents are carried into the hall. The postman now comes in the morning and afternoon and what seems to be a constant flow of carriers deliver packages. Each and all of these must have their foreignness expunged. Worse is to come. The elderly arrive early on Christmas Eve, their friendly greetings ignored as he hurries from suitcase to suitcase. Then come the teenage children who haven't seen him for months and want to pick him up, when there are rucksacks and squashy canvas bags to see to. There are mixed consolations with these arrivals. Despite my warnings, doors get left open and at last, he has access to those parts of the house previously denied him – but at a heavy price. The dining room, drawing room and the whole of the upstairs have remained neglected for so long, any vestige of previous leg cockings have long since lost their potency. Sofas, chairs, valances and acres of curtain bottoms must be attended to without delay and then, once everyone has unpacked, there are all those shoes...

Periodically he is caught in the act and finds himself shut back in the gunroom – a terrible mistake on someone's part, when so much has yet to be done. A terrier thwarted in the performance of his duties is not a happy dog and the house reverberates to a repertoire of unearthly shrieks, until the inevitable cry of 'Let Tug out, before he eats a hole in the door!' allows him to get on with the job in hand. After all, a large box of decorations which hasn't seen the light of day for nearly a year has just appeared, badly in need of a canine touch-up and a pile of coloured parcels has accumulated round the Christmas tree, some of which were wrapped elsewhere. These, too, must have a little golden droplet. Just as Tug feels he's making a fist of things, a team of carol singers arrives from the village. This merry band have already been to other farms in the valley and as they lift their faces skyward to bellow the festive hymns, Tug is hard at work on trouser-leg and gumboot.

What with frantic, last minute wrappings-up, the household is always late to bed, but on Christmas morning Tug is off round his boundaries again. By now lack of sleep is making him confused and once back in the house, he feels the need to check that nothing has been overlooked. The dining and drawing rooms will be closed at that hour, but up above, the young are opening their stockings. Filled with the spirit of the occasion and entirely misinterpreting his presence in their bedrooms, he is rewarded with edibles from Santa Claus. There are more treats and possibly a strange handbag or two carelessly left unattended, when presents round the tree are opened at midday. Christmas lunch is always a lengthy affair and although he periodically bustles off on a business of his own, instinct brings him back when the plates are cleared and turkey scraps or fat from the Bradenham are his by Christmas tradition. With the crackers, he abandons his natural reserve and plays his party piece: barking furiously round the table and savaging the empty wrappers. He is even prepared to suffer the indignity of a paper hat.

About tea-time, exhausted and bloated with food, Tug and I retire to my office for a few moments of tranquillity. As I slump in an armchair, the old man clambers on to my knee. He's a dog who never complains, seeks praise or affection, but now he puts his forepaws on either side of my neck and licks my eyelids. 'I've done my best for you,' he seems to say. 'I've sung for my supper and every room in the house is now secure. Couldn't you get rid of everyone?' At that particular moment there is nothing I could wish for more.

Keep the Home Fires Burning

At the second Council of Tours, in AD 567, it was decreed that any cleric found in bed with his wife should be excommunicated for a year and reduced to the lay state; that monks were forbidden to sleep two to a bed; and that the twelve days from the Nativity to Epiphany should be a work-free period of religious celebration. The last part of the decree became English law in AD 877 and was, of course, the early Church endeavouring to impose Christian beliefs on the ancient pagan festival of Yule, the time of great winter solstitial celebrations. Primitive man would light ritual bonfires to rejoice in the sun's rebirth and make sacrifices to the fertility goddess, Freyja.

From the Middle Ages, until a ban was imposed during the Commonwealth, the Twelve Days of Christmas were a national period of feasting, merry-making and charitable hospitality, culminating on Twelfth Night. Many aspects of the festival were revived after the Reformation and since then – although contemporary Christmas has gradually evolved from a combination of existing customs, outside influences and astute commercialisation – the historical element of a work-free period at Christmastide remains unchanged.

These twelve days have become a remarkable phenomenon. They are the only period in the course of a year when the whole Christian world is on leave at the same time. The manic pressure of business stutters to a halt. The incessant telephone calls cease to intrude; the mailbox on the computer lies empty and, unlike normal holidays, there is none of the anxiety about commitments piling up in one's absence. For some, the battle of school runs and finding time to attend children's sports fixtures is, for a blessed moment, a thing of the past. The fever of life, which dominates most people's day from dawn to dusk and reaches a climax in the run-up to Christmas Day, slows to a manageable pace. There is tranquillity and peace, the most important word in the Christmas message.

In recent years it has become fashionable in certain circles to go abroad immediately after Christmas, abandoning the dank winter climate and short days of Britain, for African sunshine or Alpine snow. This has always struck me as the most extraordinary thing to do. Why go to all the trouble of preparing for Christmas in the usual way, with decorations, food and presents, all of which are intended to be enjoyed at leisure, and then exchange them for the nightmare of air travel and the dubious pleasures of a foreign holiday? Why do this when every year at home, regardless of the weather, Christmastide gives us that most valuable of all commodities: time.

For many of us, the last six days of the Old year and the first six of the New, offer a rare occasion when the young are at home and the family is able to spend time together. These are the bright faces seen at the Boxing Day meet or on a day's shooting, bringing the joy of their youth and energy to the season. There is the pleasure of meeting old friends, whilst the Christmas ham and cold spiced beef provide an easy opportunity to be hospitable, in the true tradition of the Twelve Days. There is time, too, to be considerate and make the effort – no doubt long deferred – to pay a call on someone who would appreciate the visit.

There is time to pick a gun out of the cupboard, stick a handful of cartridges in a pocket and take the terriers for a jolly along a hedgerow; or to stand under a tree in the late afternoon waiting for pigeons to flight in to roost; perhaps to listen to leaves rustling in the wind and watch sheep on a distant hillside move slowly to their high ground. Nature has a strange atmosphere of calm expectancy about her at this time of year. It is almost as if wildlife and even the plants and trees can sense what we cannot see: that the wheel of the seasons has turned and, although we are still in deep midwinter, the hours of daylight with their promise of spring are imperceptibly getting longer.

Christmastide provides the freedom to sit in an armchair by a crackling fire, with the rain lashing at the window, and read a book or play cards as a family, in the way we used to when the children were small. Or simply watch the flames dance hypnotically among the logs and allow one's thoughts to drift uninterrupted. These priceless moments of quiet reflection are when we remember the past and think about our hopes for the coming year. They are the gift of the Twelve Days of Christmas and ought to be cherished. You won't find them on a beach in Cape Town or the slopes of Val d'Isère.

Lang may yer lum reek.

The Countryman's Zimmer

January gives us the depths of bleak midwinter; the gradual change in the weather cycle is more noticeable now than at any other time. Thirty years ago in the Borders, a heavy fall of snow was inevitable. Now, we can expect anything from bitter, iron-hard frost, driving rain and a freezing east wind that takes the skin off your face, to temperatures warm enough to tempt puzzled winter sleepers from their hibernacula. Regardless of the weather, I do love the stark beauty of January: the bare, leafless trees, their naked branches reaching for grey, brooding, winter skies, the heavy silence of woodland and the musty smell of decaying leaves.

There is a wood of hazel, birch and willows growing on a steep bank above the Liddel Water not far from the farmhouse, which is a favourite place of mine. I always go there at this time of year, not only to cut hazel shanks for the ram's-horn-leg crooks I use on the farm but also to look for a suitable thumb-stick. Hazel grows throughout Britain. It is a natural understorey found in oak and ash woodland, in hedgerows that have been left to grow and along stream banks. Thousands of hectares of hazel were once coppiced for fencing stobs, hurdles, barrel staves, broomsticks, clothes-pegs, ties for fastening thatch and (before bamboo) fishing rods. The wood was burnt extensively to provide charcoal for gunpowder and the nuts were a valuable source of winter protein and carbohydrates.

Up until the end of the 1930s, it was common practice for schools in villages and market towns to close on Holy Rood or Nutting Day, 14th September, to allow children to join their parents gathering nuts. Until fairly recently, there was a charming Scots custom where courting couples each chose a hazelnut and placed them in the embers of a fire on Hallowe'en. If the nuts burnt together, it was the sign of eternal true love; if one of the nuts exploded, it was an indication that the person who had chosen the nut was being unfaithful and that the relationship was doomed.

Nowadays, few people bother to go nutting; and apart from a handful of artisans still making hurdles, most hazel is cut as shanks by professional stick-makers, who sell armfuls every year at game fairs and county shows. The most attractive hazel for stick-making, with beautiful silvery bark, is found on rocky soil through the west of the country and particularly in Scotland. The old Gaelic word for hazel is cuil, coll, cal or even cow, as in Cowglen, and it appears frequently in place names in the west of Scotland; the Isle of Coll, for example, or Bar Calltuin in Appin. It is the origin of the name of the Clan Colquhoun, whose badge is the hazel, and the Roman name for Scotland, Caledonia, comes from Cal-Dun, which means Hill of Hazel.

Of all the aids to locomotion, a thumb-stick is by far the most useful, particularly after one reaches the age when the consequences of all those hours spent lying in muddy creeks waiting for the dawn flight or wearing sodden clothes on wet hunting days begin to take effect. A good thumb-stick combines two roles: it propels one forward over rough, steep or muddy ground and also supports the weight of the body when standing for any length of time. Stick-makers sell any number at shows, but nothing compares to the pleasure of a thumb-stick one has made oneself.

A shank should be cut when the sap is down and the bark still hard, from the beginning of November to before catkins start appearing at the end of February. January, in my view, is the optimum month. Look for a stave that will give you a shank of between four feet six inches and five feet, with a diameter no greater than an inch-and-a-half at the bottom and an inch at the point where the stave branches into a V. Balance along the length of the stick is all-important – stick-makers call a well-balanced stick 'clever'. It should be light enough to carry in comfort yet strong enough to support the body. The V must be the width of the thumb. This too is all-important as the thumb will be bearing the weight as one propels oneself along. I always look for a shank that is slightly canted forward at the V, so it will ultimately fit nicely into the palm, and I trim the V to about four inches. Don't worry if the stave is not completely straight. Hazel is pliable and can be straightened as it dries (which takes about a year), by attaching it to a beam and hanging a heavy weight from the bottom.

Once dried, the next step – and the most crucial – is cutting the shank to length. Hold your arm straight out from the shoulder, clench your fist, measure the distance from thumb to ground and add four inches. Then, cut off little bits to suit, bearing in mind the position that one finds the most relaxing when standing for any length of time. Some people, such as myself, like to place the stick in an armpit and lean into it, while others can be seen propped more or less vertical with their arms folded and the stick wedged into the fleshy part of a forearm.

Finally, you will need something to protect the point. If it is going to get a lot of use, an empty 12-bore cartridge will do the job but I find this too noisy for stalking. I prefer an inch-and-a-half piece of one-eighth copper piping, slightly smaller than the diameter of the stick, which I whittle down to fit into it. A dab of glue and the countryman's Zimmer is ready to go.

Hedge Pig

The old cart shed, part of the slate-roofed steading that forms a square round the cobbled yard behind the house, has been used for years as a log store. Through autumn and winter a substantial pile of detritus builds up in one of the corners as bark and wood chips are shovelled clear of the splitting block. The terrier pups have convinced themselves that something interesting must be hidden in the depths of the heap and, until they get bored, any log-splitting exercise is accompanied by frenzied digging. Their efforts were finally rewarded one day, when they discovered a hedgehog that must have come out of its winter torpor when the temperature dropped below freezing and relocated under the chip pile.

Towards the end of autumn, hedgehogs start searching for suitable sites to construct individual hibernacula, thick nests of leaves and grass. These may be inside compost heaps, under brush wood, deep among the roots of a hedge, in old rabbit burrows or wasps' nests and beneath garden sheds. When there is a sustained period of low temperature in November, December or January and the food source of invertebrates becomes more difficult to find, hedgehogs retreat to their hibernacula. They become torpid, their bodies cool from thirty-five degrees to ten. Heartbeat rate drops from around a hundred and ninety per minute to a scarcely perceptible twenty. Respiration is reduced to once every few minutes and they survive on energy from body fat built up over the summer. Fluctuations in temperature cause them to wake up, particularly extreme cold. If the glass falls below freezing, the hedgehog's metabolism switches back on again, his body temperature rises and, rather than improve the insulation in an existing hibernaculum, he will look for an alternative site.

Hibernation lasts until late March or April and sufficient body weight in early winter is vital. A young hedgehog under five hundred grams or an adult weighing less than a kilogram is unlikely to survive.

Mating begins as soon as they have recovered from hibernation and lasts until July, with the boar travelling up to three kilometres a night in search of a sow. Apart from a snuffling sound when quartering the ground in search of food and a mewing which the young make when frightened, mating is a rare occasion when the creatures become vocal. During the witch scene in *Macbeth*, 'thrice and once the hedge-pig whin'd' refers to the boar calling for a sow. Courtship is protracted and involves much circling, snorting and bumping as the boar encourages the sow to flatten her spines and protrude her hindquarters, allowing him to mate without risk of injury. As soon as mating is over, the boar abandons the sow and sets off in search of another.

Gestation takes between four and five weeks, with the sow usually giving birth to five piglets. The young are born blind with a coat of soft white spines which are beneath the skin to protect the mother during birth, emerging after a few hours. These are replaced by a second coat of stronger spines after thirty-six hours, followed by a third and darker adult set, which develop into a protective layer of between five and six thousand spines twenty-five millimetres long. Each spine lasts about a year before dropping off and being replaced by a fresh one. The face and belly are covered in coarse hair and, unable to groom themselves, their coats are usually full of fleas and mites. Young hedgehogs' eyes open at ten days; they can curl into a defensive ball at a fortnight; and are weaned after four weeks, then learning to forage at night with their mothers. At six weeks they become independent.

A sow disturbed with a litter of newborn young often kills or abandons them, but will transport older ones by the scruff to a safer place. A sow that has lost a litter may come in season again and have another, but the young will be unlikely to gain enough body weight to last the winter.

Hedgehogs spend all day asleep in a secluded nest, emerging to feed after dark and covering about ninety thousand square metres hunting for the hundred or so invertebrates required to satisfy their appetite. They are only seen by day when food is scarce or if their body weight is low as winter approaches. A hedgehog's diet consists mainly of worms, beetles and caterpillars, but it will also eat berries, fallen fruit, slugs, snails, eggs and fledglings of small, ground-nesting birds, mice, frogs, lizards and carrion.

In a dry summer I have often seen hedgehogs at night feeding on road kill. They are immune to adder bites and are reputed to eat them, having first provoked the adder into exhausting itself attacking their impenetrable wall of spines. They have notoriously feeble eyesight, relying on acute senses of smell and hearing to locate prey above ground and up to three centimetres below the soil surface. They can swim and climb and are capable of reaching astonishing speeds for short periods.

Furze pigs, urchins or hedge pigs, as they are still known by some country people, are incredibly ancient in evolutionary terms and have been foraging across Britain and Europe from Scandinavia to Romania for over ten million years. For much of their association with humans they have been victims of prejudice and either killed for food and quack medicine or treated as vermin.

The Romans were partial to hedgehog and the easily digested boiled flesh was a popular invalid food in the Middle Ages. Hedgehog meat was frequently eaten by country people well into the last century and the fat was reputed to cure all manner of ills – from boils to baldness. There was a widely held and persistent belief that they stole milk from cows and spread the dreaded murrain among cattle. In 1566 they were declared vermin under the Act for the Preservation of Grain and a bounty was paid by church wardens for the snouts of hedgehogs killed in their parish. This Act was only repealed in 1863, but by then they were being persecuted by gamekeepers for stealing game bird eggs. There was also a brisk trade in live hedgehogs at London's Leadenhall

Market, where they were bought to control cockroaches and other insects in cellars, larders and food stores.

Under the UK Biodiversity Action Plan, hedgehogs are currently listed as a species of conservation concern: a status I suspect will soon become a priority. A phenomenal number die on the roads, while others are killed by garden pesticides, mowing machines and manmade pitfalls such as swimming pools, cattle grids, steep-sided drains, rubbish and plastic netting. But the single greatest threat to them is badgers. Badgers and hedgehogs share the same woodland habitat and as badger numbers escalate every year, the hedgehog population is declining. A hedgehog's spines are no protection against a hungry brock and the one among my woodchips is the first I have seen in this part of the world for a long time. Once the terriers had been called off and kennelled, on this occasion I took the tightly curled little bundle and pushed it deep into a hay stack. With luck, it would survive the rest of the winter.

The Glorious Bird
of Colchis

January can be an unsettling month; the hours of daylight are imperceptibly lengthening, yet spring is a long way off. If the wind blows from the east, we could have a heavy fall of snow at any time or weeks of iron-hard frost, bringing hunting to a stop and a ban on estuary shooting. Equally, the bitter, hungry wind could suddenly turn to the west; temperatures then rise dramatically, snowdrops and winter aconites emerge, hibernants stumble blearily from their hibernacula and on flooded water meadows, adjacent to salt marshes, snipe congregate in such numbers that they resemble clouds of midges. I always think the best aspect of January is that pheasants are stronger, higher, wilder, faster and better eating than those shot before Christmas; for an unpredictable and sporting bird, a high, wide, long-crossing January scorcher is very hard to beat.

It always amuses me, when I see a crafty old late-season cock sneaking out of the corner of a beat, to reflect on the fact that no other bird has been so frequently portrayed as synonymous with the British countryside and yet he is a complete stranger. The bird we know as the Old English black-neck originated – according to the Athenian historian Aeschylus, writing in the fifth century BC – from the marshes beside the River Phasis in the kingdom of Colchis, now part of Georgia. *Phasianus colchicus* arrived here via Ancient Greece with the Romans in AD 43, as a table bird. For the next five hundred years, the ancestors of the modern pheasant lived a life of pampered domesticity, appearing as delicacies at patrician banquets dressed in all their glorious plumage.

Palladius, in his *Opus agriculturae*, gave instructions on their care and feeding: chicks should be fed on boiled grains sprinkled with wine for the first fortnight, before moving to a more robust diet of ants' eggs mixed with flour and olive oil. The collapse of the Empire would have been a severe shock to those birds that were left behind, but somehow enough survived among the ruins of their former homes to breed the nucleus of a feral population.

The Saxons and Danes were hopeless historians and the earliest evidence of the naturalisation of pheasants is a regulation of Earl Harold, written in 1059, allowing the canons of Waltham Abbey in Essex the choice of a brace of partridge or a pheasant as a privilege of their office. The Normans imported more pheasants as part of their living larders and thereafter, these vain, supercilious, quarrelsome creatures appear regularly in historical records, strutting across the centuries, insouciantly rubbing shoulders with the great and the good.

Classified as Fowls of Warren under the Forest Laws, the right to keep and kill pheasants were in the King's gift, doled out as privileges to the nobility or clergy. Their rarity and demand as a delicacy at medieval banquets ensured documentation unique to pheasants and from this we know that Bishop Rudolphus presented the monks of Rochester with sixteen in 1089; that Henry I granted the Abbot of Amesbury the right to keep pheasants in 1100; that Thomas à Becket had just dined off one when he was murdered in Canterbury Cathedral and that 200 were eaten at the magnificent enthronement feast for George Neville, Archbishop of York, in 1465.

Prices were scrupulously recorded; fourpence (4d) in 1299 had risen to one shilling (1s) by 1512, with a massive leap to two shillings and eightpence (2s 8d) by the middle of the century. Henry VIII was so partial to pheasant that he engaged the services of a French priest as his personal pheasant keeper, paying him out of the Privy Purse expenses.

Pheasants were no less revered in medieval France. The Duke of Burgundy hosted an eighteen-day extravaganza in 1454, known as the Banquet of The Oath of the Pheasant, at which the finest flower of

French knighthood swore a solemn oath, over a bejewelled and gilded pheasant, to follow the Duke on a crusade against the Turks.

A bird of woodland fringes, in Great Britain *Phasianus colchicus* remained scarce and localised until the Agricultural Revolution and the Enclosure Acts provided improved food sources and thousands of miles of quick-set hedging as cover. Shooting flying birds had become commonplace by the mid-eighteenth century and the sport of shooting hedgerow pheasants led to the development of a new breed of gundog – the Springer spaniel. More habitat was created during the agricultural depression following the Battle of Waterloo as landlords, sensing the potential in establishing cover for game, planted trees on pockets of poor quality arable land. The pheasant population was expanding rapidly and with the development of Forsyth's percussion cap, pheasants were being driven to guns for the first time on Lord Leicester's Holkham Estate in Norfolk by about 1840. With the rationalisation of the old, restrictive game laws, shooting became increasingly popular among wealthy Victorians and the development of the railways made it accessible to them.

By 1860, gunmaker Joseph Lang had improved Lefaucheux's breech loading action, enabling guns to shoot as fast as they were able to load Eley's new composite cartridge. Thus driven shooting became all the rage. Landlords experimented with different breeds of pheasant – Japanese, Chinese and Mongolian – to find a hardy bird that flew well and held to its ground; whilst also devoting time and money to creating coverts to encourage birds to fly high and fast between woods. This woodland planting for pheasant habitat not only shaped the landscape we know today, but provided us with a conservation legacy which now covers two million hectares of land and benefits all birdlife: something the RSPB is quick to forget.

Marl

On the last day of the inland wildfowling season, 31st January, I was crouched among reeds on the edge of an old, flooded marl pit, looking across the Tweed Valley and the looming bulk of the Cheviots, in the forlorn hope that a trip of teal might drop in to feed. It was a still, windless evening, too soft for duck, and as my concentration ebbed, I began to ponder on the labour which must have gone in to digging marl pits and the lengths to which our farming forefathers went, to improve the land and increase its fertility.

Marl is formed from the soft concentrations of secondary calcium carbonate and clay; it was created at the end of the last Ice Age and is to be found in swathes along the contour lines of the slopes formed by retreating ice. No one knows exactly how early agriculturalists discovered that spreading clay on sandy ground enriched the soil and improved its capacity to hold nutrients and water, but writing in 70 AD, the Roman historian, Pliny the Elder, observed that this was common practice among the Celts.

Marling became widespread across Britain after the Norman Invasion and continued in general use well into the nineteenth century, with the marl traditionally dug out of the ground and spread in February. Modern agriculture has destroyed the vast proportion of the thousands of marl pits that were once a feature of the landscape, but the few that remain beside ancient permanent pastures are easily recognisable by the shallow, sloping, squared edge at one end of their elongated length and the deep, broad, rounded shape at the other. Marl is found at between one and three yards depth and the shape was formed by several hundredweights of marl being dug out and loaded into carts, which were then hauled up the sloping end of the pit, a process which was repeated time and again. Over twelve months the pit would fill with water and another would be dug nearby the following February, eventually creating a little cluster of perfect flight ponds.

Land close to towns, villages, religious communities and manors was enriched with a staggering variety of fertilising material; human waste ('night soil'), and all household refuse, soot, ash, the residue of the pigeon dung after the lye had been extracted, malt waste, rags, shreds of leather from leather works, the detritus of tanneries; offal and blood from slaughter-houses, horn trimmings from the manufacture of spoons, knife handles and drinking vessels, hoof refuse from glue works, plus wine lees mixed with wood ash. Land near the sea had the benefit of fish guts from the catches of fishing fleets, chalk, sand, river mud, sea sludge and seaweed, both wet and burnt, whilst in the limestone counties, such as Derbyshire, lime was quarried, burnt and spread to reduce acidity in the soil.

One of the reasons marling remained so popular and widespread in rural areas was the lack of natural fertiliser, as much of the livestock was traditionally slaughtered and salted in the autumn, due to a limited and uncertain supply of over-wintering food sources. The nucleus of breeding stock that remained was taken inside and littered on ferns, bracken or reeds, but left little in the way of bedding dung. Marl remained effective in the soil for as long as twelve years, but more importantly, where fields had been marled it was unnecessary to follow the customary practice of leaving one fallow for a season to restore its fertility.

The heyday of marling was in the early part of the Agricultural Revolution and main thrust of the Enclosure Acts, when three million acres of common land, mostly heath, moor or fen, were enclosed and improved to meet the demands of an escalating population.

Even though marl was free and easily accessible, by the middle of the nineteenth century marling was dying out, a victim in some respects of its own success. The introduction of fodder crops from the Continent meant more stock could now be over-wintered, providing a constant supply of natural manure. Transport became revolutionised as canals were dug and roads metalled, making lime and the coal to burn it readily available, with lime kilns proliferating across the country where marl had previously been dug.

In particular, agricultural improvements, both rapid advances in technology and better farm management, led to a steady annual drop in the numbers of employees, as farm labour was used more efficiently or replaced by machinery. By 1850, only twenty-two per cent of the British workforce was employed in agriculture; the smallest proportion for any country in the world at the time. Extracting, hauling and spreading marl was a long, slow, time-consuming job and with available labour now in short supply, as much of the displaced rural population sought work in the growing industrial towns, marling ceased to be cost-effective.

February is still the traditional month for fertilising. At this time of the year farms in the valley below will start feeding the land for spring growth, as farmers have done for many millennia. Walking back to the car, I reflected on what an extraordinary creation our landscape is; it is impossible to go from one district to another without coming across some arresting reminder of the country's ancient past. A stone circle, an Iron Age fort, traces of rig and furrow ploughing, a sunken lane, a circular stell, castle or abbey ruins, lime kiln or marl pit – even an isolated patch of nettles – indicate that humans had once settled in the immediate vicinity. Each enchanting surprise opens a little window of history.